Y0-DKL-529

FACE TO FACE . . .
WITH YOURSELF

FACE TO FACE... WITH YOURSELF

CHARLES L. MCKAY

BROADMAN PRESS
Nashville, Tennessee

4252-35
ISBN: 0-8054-5235-4

Library of Congress Catalog Card Number: 75-27410
Dewey Decimal Classification: 220.92
Subject Headings: Bible - Biography // Christian Life
Printed in the United States of America

DEDICATION

To the young people of First Southern Baptist Church of Scottsdale, Arizona, who helped me conceive the idea

To the college students in my class at California Baptist College who encouraged the work

To my four grandchildren who are youth:

To young people and adults across the land who desire to know and do the will of God, this book is dedicated.

Preface

Face to Face with Yourself was born during a series of rap sessions between the pastor and his young people of the First Southern Baptist Church, Scottsdale, Arizona.

These rap sessions were simple, down-to-earth, Bible studies that lasted for two hours every Tuesday night for several months.

In prayer, searching for the sort of Bible study we could do together that would be of most help to our young people, the idea was born.

From several in the group, the idea kept coming up; "If we could make these sessions such that they would be helpful to young people in the areas of *choice-making* and *problem-solving*, we would be happy."

With this in mind, each one in the group agreed to select two characters each from the Bible, make a thorough study and in turn a character analysis of each would be made. We followed this simple procedure. Each young person selected one Bible character that he or she would desire to be like—a good character. Then he chose a character that he would not desire to be like—a bad character. For this reason, *Face to Face . . . with Yourself* has in it, personalities both good and bad.

These kids dug keep into the Bible, and every other available source, for facts concerning their characters. We took one and sometimes two characters at each session. The facts concerning the Bible character were related to the group, after which the entire group made a detailed analysis of the character. We literally took the person apart from head to toe to see what made him tick. An effort was made to find the reason for every choice he made during his entire life. These decisions were followed up to find their end results.

If the choice and the results were right and good, we discussed how people could benefit by these lessons. If the choices were wrong and the results bad, we determined to profit by the mistakes the person had made.

From the Bible record of every character, we searched for his weak points, his strong points, the mistakes he made, and how it could have been different had a different choice been made at the time.

The entire study was for us to take a look at ourselves in the light of the Bible character we analyzed. The Bible study, using Bible characters as mirrors through which we could see ourselves, produced changed lives to the degree that it became self-evident in the homes and in the church.

Before long the adults asked for the privilege of sharing in the study sessions.

We continued this approach on Sunday and Wednesday nights over an extended period. Since then, I have tried this with our college students. It works. I commend it.

Charles L. McKay
Professor of Bible
California Baptist College
Riverside, California

CONTENTS

Suggestions for Using This Book

Church groups, large or small, could meet at regularly scheduled periods with the pastor or another convenor delegated with the responsibility of leading the group.

A member of the class could agree in advance of each meeting to present the character to be studied during the session.

If the class is large, after presenting all the facts of the person, break up into small groups. Four to each group is ideal. After sufficient time has been given each group to make a character analysis—with suggestions that each person could learn from the study—the entire group will come back together.

Someone should report for each group. It would be helpful if one would compile the lessons gleaned and provide a copy for each member—perhaps at the next class session.

The analysis at the conclusion of each chapter is only suggestive, to give some idea of the possibilities for group study.

The book is designed so any person can read it alone without group study. For individual study you should have a pencil and sheet of paper handy. As soon as you read the chapter, you can make your own personal analysis; then take a careful look at yourself.

FACE TO FACE . . .
WITH YOURSELF

Introduction

Most emotionally maladjusted people are so because they are not willing to accept themselves as they are. Rather than accept their limitations or their lot in life, they had rather be someone else. But being someone else is impossible. Come face to face . . . with yourself because you are the one person with whom you must learn to live.

You are the one person from whom you can never get a divorce. You cannot escape yourself. With yourself, you must live. You, forever, *have yourself on your hands.*

Planes take off against their opposition, the wind. The healthy person is one who visualizes in his handicaps a bundle of possibilities for good and channels them for the best. A World War I veteran, a well-known aviation expert, testified that he owed his successful and happy career to losing a leg in the service. His happiness came, not in spite of his disability, but because of it. What others called the end to his career, this major in the air force claimed as a bright and new beginning.

All too many people spend their time making life a failure, when the same amount of time rightly used would spell success and happiness. Marcus Aurelius kept before himself the motto: "Do not act as if you had a thousand years to live."

Thackeray remarked that the world is a looking glass which gives back to every man the reflection of his own face. Are you one of those persons highly allergic to yourself? Do you fear being alone? Are you afraid to be by yourself? Have you started working at being what you are capable of becoming? Is life to you really worth living? If, while you read the chapters of this book, you will take a look at yourself in the light of what you could become, your time will have been spent for good. If this book becomes a mirror through which you see yourself as you are, and if it helps you to determine that you will strive to be someday, what you are capable of becoming, then your reading time will not have been in vain. It is the desire and purpose of the author to present these Bible characters in such a way that his readers will profit by both the mistakes and the good points of each. Purposefully, the contents of the book are more illustrative than explanatory—for you see, illustrations enable people to fathom truths that otherwise they would miss.

Someone has said that living is at least 90 percent attitude; therefore, life is what you make it. The Bible says, "As [a man] thinketh in his heart, so is he" (Prov. 23:7). In other words, you have become or you are becoming what you think or have been thinking. If you are dissatisfied with your lot in life, then as you read this book keep one thought in mind: "You need not stay the way you are." You can begin to become what you ought to be. If life to you is worthwhile, it is not because you found it that way; it is because you helped make it what it is. Christian faith offers and challenges every life to become more than a conqueror, no matter what the circumstances may be.

As you read about the characters in this book—some of which were complete failures, while others lived zestfully and successfully—you will discover that happy and successful people live daily under discipline and submission to the will of God. The good life is a series of disciplines. One of Holman Hunt's greatest admirers asked him how she might become an artist like him. His reply to her was, "All you need to do, dear lady, is to practice eight hours every day for forty years." To do this you must have a vision that gives direction and purpose to your life.

Those who knew him best said of Paderewski that he thought nothing of going over a single bar of music forty times before he was satisfied with how he played it. After the great musician had played for Queen Victoria, she enthusiastically exulted, "Mr. Paderewski, you are a genius," to which he replied, "But before I was a genius, I was a drudge."

It is the prayer of this author that those who read this book will not put it down without vision, direction, and purpose that will result in deeper meaning to life.

If you will, live with these characters until you eliminate the company of those you desire not to imitate, and adopt as companions and examples those you would like to emulate. Then walk in their company until you have discovered their dreams, their faith, their purpose in life, and the manner by which they achieved their purpose. Search for their secret.

On the fifth anniversary of the death of Calvin Coolidge Jr., his mother wrote these words: "You, my son, have shown me God. Your kiss upon my cheek has made me feel the gentle touch of him who leads us on."

Self-knowledge precedes self-improvement. The story is told that in the battle with the Saracens in Spain, the Scots threw the heart of Robert the Bruce ahead, and then fought their way with all their might to follow it. The challenge did it. The fellow who makes the most out of life sets for himself a challenging, worthy goal, throws it out ahead, and fights with all his might to achieve it. Life, to be worthy, must be organized and lived around a basic purpose. Life is not something to be found; it is something to create.

Direction is so important and all too many people flounder around more years than necessary before they discover the importance of direction for their lives. Margaret Mitchell knew where she was going and the goal she planned to achieve in *Gone With the Wind* before she wrote the book. She had a vision of the finished product, and she wrote the last chapter before the others were written. Edison had a vision of one day becoming an inventor. Florence Nightingale dreamed of being a nurse in her future. Such purpose and direction give meaning to life. Alexander Hamilton once declared, "Men, give me credit for some genius. All the genius I have lies in this: when I have a subject at hand, I study it profoundly. Day and night, it is before me. My mind becomes pervaded with it. Then the effort which I have made is what people are pleased to call the fruit of genius. It is the fruit of labor and thought."

Someone wrote the sad but truthful words, "If the world loses any of its worth, it is because some of us take from it more than we give." This was true of the college girl who wrote in her college annual in 1919: "I don't bother work and it don't bother me." It is no wonder that a few years later the college newspaper carried her life's story which revealed her death by suicide. This dear girl had no purpose in life, and no vision and faith through which she could lay hold on the real reason for living.

I like the watchword of the late President of the United States, John F. Kennedy: "Ask not what your country can do for you, rather ask what you can do for your country."

Dear reader, your basic purpose in life speaks. It says, "I am the image you want to make real." A careful study of the characters of this book should help you determine what to do and how to do it to make your purpose a reality. As you read the lives of these characters, fix the image you want for yourself ten, twenty, even fifty years ahead. If you will do this, and at the same time–in the will of God–let your objective become the automatic pilot, it will get you there.

Once you have done this, you must realize that there could be several ways of achieving your purpose, but you must decide on a specific plan and follow it.

The old adage is true. "If you think you can't then you are right: you can't. But if you think you can, you are right, for you can." Many Americans who fail in life never realize that the last four letters of American are "I can."

Benjamin Franklin decided early in his life that the reason so many people fail is because they have no plan. They muddle through life, hoping for the best and usually getting the worst. David Starr Jordan said many times, "The world turns aside to let any man pass who knows where he is going." When asked to what he attributed his success, J. L. Kraft, the cheese manufacturer replied, "It is my ability to make up my mind." Mr. Kraft knew where he was going, and he knew how he planned to get there.

If you pluck only one pearl from this cluster, let it be that the characters that disappointed you also disappointed God. The characters after whom you would like to pattern your life pleased God by making him Master of their lives. Only in God's will can one, made in the likeness and image of God, be supremely happy and gloriously content. Man cannot live happily apart from God, his Creator. Francis Thompson tried all sorts of methods to escape God, finally to be overtaken by him. He summed up his confession in *The Hound of Heaven.*

Several hundred miles from the Gulf of Mexico, far up into the mountains, there was once a tiny pool of water that a thirsty ox could drink dry. One day this tiny pool of water got homesick for the great sea. It had a dream of something better. It dreamed of the mighty ships that plowed the waters of the ocean, the huge monsters that enjoyed the freedom of the vast water area, and the great attractions of her beauty and worth to man. Able to stand its condition no longer, this tiny pool of water leaped over its rim and started down the mountainside. It leaped from one crag to another, reaching out its hands to grasp other small streams that were on their way to the sea. Ever widening and deepening, this little stream finally reached the mighty Mississippi River which carried it on out into the sea.

As you read this book, keep this story in mind and let it become a parable of your life.

1
What Selfish Ambition Will Do
(Rebekah)
Genesis 24; 25:20-34; 27

As the sun was sinking in the distance across the desert, the women from the little village of Nahor were trudging down the pathways that merged from every direction at the well. While off in the distance, winding down from the southwest, came a small caravan of camels.

Rebekah learned later that seated on one of the softfooted animals was Eliezer (Gen. 15:2), the chief steward of Abraham. Abraham was the father of the new nation, the people of God. Having felt that his end was not too far in the distant future, Abraham had committed his chief servant to a pact. Calling him in one day, he made Eliezer vow that he would not permit Isaac, the promised heir, to marry a woman of the land of Canaan. In doing so, Abraham had charged the servant to travel to the far east, Rebekah's country, to seek a wife for Isaac from among his own people, his kindred.

One other commitment Abraham had requested of his chief servant. The servant was to see that Isaac was not allowed to return to the father's homeland to live, for God had promised to Abraham and his descendants the land of Canaan. There the patriarch wanted his son of promise to live. Therefore, in keeping with his vow to perform his master's wishes, Eliezer was on his mission to find a wife for Isaac.

As the women walked around the bend in the trail, Eliezer's caravan of camels, loaded with presents for the family who would furnish the bride for Isaac, was swaying along the desert highway.

Approaching the well-site, Eliezer commanded the caravan of

camels to kneel down at the watering place. Since it was eventide, the women, carrying their water pots on their heads, were converging on the well.

Seeing them coming, Eliezer breathed a prayer that God would reveal the girl to him. This he later shared with Rebekah. In fact, he said that he had put out a "fleece." In his prayer, Eliezer prayed that one of the girls, the one the Lord had for young Isaac's bride, would respond by giving him a drink from her pot. Not only that, but he prayed that the young woman would also share some of the water with his camels. Of course, none of this the young bride-to-be knew at the time.

The girls began to draw water from the community well. We don't know how many drew water ahead of Rebekah, but several did. They put their jars back on their heads and paid no attention to the stranger who stood there wanting a drink. At last it had come her time to draw. She took her pitcher from her shoulder and something told her to give the tired stranger a drink. And she did before he could thank her. She drew water and poured it into the trough where the tired, thirsty camels had bowed.

Certain that God had answered his prayer and that his master's request had been granted, the steward took from among the presents the golden earrings and bracelets, presented them to the kind young lady. Then, he asked her name and that of her family, explaining the significance of what she had done.

Learning that Rebekah was from a family related to Abraham, Eliezer explained that he was even more pleased and certain that the Lord answered his prayer and that of his master. Evidently, Rebekah was "lovely to look at." To say the least, she was gracious and courteous, too. She had a good family background, and had been taught well. Again, the chief steward bowed his head and gave thanks to the God who had led him to a bride for his master's heir of promise. Finding out who Rebekah was and where she lived, Eliezer accompanied her home, to the house of her brother, Laban, to consummate the deal. When Eliezer made his proposal to Laban, he immediately gave his consent—with the one stipulation, that Rebekah must make the final decision for herself.

After explaining to her why the stranger had come and what his proposal was, her brother asked her: "Wilt thou go with this man?" To which Rebekah replied without hesitation, "I will go."

Laban relieved the ten camels of the rich presents brought to Rebekah's family. Then, with a night's rest behind him, Eliezer turned toward home with a wife for Isaac. The old mate-maker had his mission accomplished.

With Eliezer, Rebekah traveled from Mesopotamia down to Canaan to marry, and later to fall in love with, Isaac, a man she had never seen!

Isaac had dearly loved his mother, and she had not long been dead when Rebekah came to be his wife. Their meeting was "on this wise." Isaac had walked across the field, possibly grieving over the loss of his mother, when in the distance he saw the dust stirred up by the camel caravan as it made the last lap of the journey home.

As the caravan drew nearer to the young man, for the first time he saw the girl who was to be his wife. When she saw Isaac in the distance, Rebekah asked the chief steward, "What man is this that walketh in the field to meet us?" When she learned that it was Isaac, her future husband, Rebekah jumped from the camel and covered her face with her veil.

It might interest you to note the vivid Bible description of the scene. "And Isaac brought her into his mother's tent, and took Rebekah, and she became his wife; and he loved her, and Isaac was comforted after the death of his mother" (Gen. 24:67).

In the course of time, Rebekah gave birth to twins, Esau and Jacob. She could never forget the words of the Lord to her when the boys were born. "The elder shall serve the younger," he had said. However, Isaac loved Esau because he was the outdoor type. Esau was a hunter, and his father loved venison and other game from the fields. Rebekah could see a vast difference in the two children, and she could not help favoring Jacob, who was much more refined than his older brother, Esau.

Seeing that Esau had a poor sense of values, Jacob soon

traded him out of his birthright. In addition to that stupid act, Esau married Judith, a Hittite woman. This was too much for his parents, especially his mother.

Rebekah had higher ambitions for her sons. Jehovah had warned against non-Hebrews marrying into the family of Israel. This was a bitter blow when their eldest disobeyed and brought reproach to them. Esau had sinned against everything Jehovah had commanded Abraham and his descendants. The future of the nation was at stake. If Jacob had also done such a foolish thing, their lives would have been in vain. To Isaac, Rebekah said, "I am weary of my life, because of the daughters of the Hittites . . . what good shall my life do to me?" Realizing that a similar thing could happen to Jacob, Rebekah set out to avoid it.

Noticing that Isaac was becoming more feeble all the time, Rebekah began to lay plans to see that her dream would come true. Isaac's daily walk outside the black tent got shorter by the day. Soon he would be confined to his tent, and Rebekah knew it. The time must come shortly for the father to bestow his double blessing upon his eldest son. She had to be ready if her plans were to work. This conniving mother lost no time, and she watched for the opportunity to accomplish her purpose.

In those days, the patriarchal blessing was of inestimable value. The eldest son usually received a double portion of his father's goods. When Esau married the heathen woman against God's will, Rebekah thought she had a right to feel that Esau had forfeited his right to this special blessing. And, too, in a fair and square deal, Esau had actually sold his birthright to his younger brother. Therefore, Rebekah could see no harm in having the double portion, the patriarchal blessing, bestowed upon Jacob. She felt he deserved it, and would use it with honor. She also had another grievance to expose. Isaac, on one occasion while passing through the territory of the Philistines, had passed her off as his sister. He was afraid that he would be killed, and Rebekah had never been able to forget that act of cowardice on Isaac's part. Now, she thought, was her opportunity to get even with him. (See Gen. 26:7.)

The time had come when Isaac was ready to bestow the blessing on his favorite son. He called Esau to his bedside. Rebekah was taking no chances. So, she hid behind the flap of the tent and listened to the instructions. She heard Isaac tell Esau to take his bow and arrow and kill a deer, and to prepare him a last meal of venison.

Soon, Esau was off on the hunt. When she knew that he was fully out of sight, Rebekah immediately called Jacob. She explained to him his father's plan and her counter scheme. Then, Jacob was to rush into the barn, kill two kid goats, and Rebekah would prepare Isaac's last meal before Esau could return from his hunt in the field. Blind Isaac could not tell the difference in the meal, Rebekah felt certain. Rebekah had assurance that her plan would work.

This much Jacob could grasp. But Esau was a hairy man. Suppose Isaac would ask to feel of him, what then? Rebekah seemed to have all of the answers. She assured Jacob that her plans would take care of that matter, too. She told him that the curse would be upon her, and for him to obey her voice.

When the young goats were prepared, Rebekah hurriedly wrapped the hands of Jacob with the skin. Then, she put the skin on the back of his neck. Thus, the plot was carried out. Jacob appeared with a delicious meal.

Isaac's ears were not as defective as his eyes. So, when Jacob entered the tent, saluted his blind father and presented the meat, Isaac faced two difficulties. First, the time seemed too short for Esau to have hunted down a deer and prepared it for eating. Second, the voice sounded like the voice of Jacob.

Undecided as to which of his sons had presented the meal, Isaac said, "Come near, my son. Let me be sure that you are my eldest son, Esau." When the trembling hands of Isaac touched the hands of Jacob, he felt the hair. Not quite satisfied, he put his feeble hands on the back of Jacob's neck, at which time he felt certain that, though it was Jacob's voice, it was Esau's hands. Still hiding behind the flap of Isaac's tent, Rebekah saw that her plan was working.

When Isaac was satisfied that it must be Esau, Isaac had Jacob bow before him. Isaac placed his hands over the younger son's head and bestowed the blessing upon him. It had come to pass. Jacob had received the double portion that ordinarily went to the eldest son. Rebekah had succeeded in her plot. Her dream had come to fruition.

She congratulated Jacob as he came from the tent of his father. She luxuriated in the success of her trickery. She had overheard the conversation between Isaac and Jacob, and was pleased with the results.

The official blessing had no sooner ended when Esau came in from the field with his father's venison. When he presented the meat to his father, and then asked for his blessing, the startled old man cried out: "Who art thou?" When Esau explained that he was indeed Isaac's firstborn son, they both knew what had happened.

Realizing the consequences, Esau begged for a portion of the blessing for himself. In tears he sought a blessing, yet "he found no place for repentance." Esau knew that earlier in life he had sold his birthright, and that he was reaping the harvest of his stupidity. "A mess of pottage," a small thing—for that moment of self-gratification he had paid an expensive price.

What Isaac had done to Jacob was irrevocable. It could not be withdrawn. However, it did not mean that Esau would not take vengeance on his brother. He declared that he would. Rebekah and Jacob knew that he meant it.

Fearing the fury of Esau, they had to devise another plan. It was to send Jacob away to the country of Rebekah's brother, Laban. She did so to get her favorite son safely away from an outraged Esau, and to make certain that he would not marry a heathen woman. This mother bade good-bye to her favorite son, never again to see him on earth, for she would experience death before Jacob would return thirty years later. A terrible price for a mother to pay—but she had to pay it.

Linda: Where there is pure, unselfish love, there will be plenty to go around for all the members of the family, no matther how many are involved. A mother who does not love all of her children is unworthy of them.

Sandra: The homes that I know where happiness has first place, there is faithfulness, loyalty, love, trust, confidence, and understanding between the husband and wife. As the Bible says, they must be *one.* There should be no grievous differences between the man and the woman in the home. This was not true in the case of Isaac and Rebekah. In our study, we have seen the tragic outcome when this isn't there.

Carl: Each person in a home is an individual and must be treated and accepted as such. We are all different. Jacob and Esau had different personalities. They were different in likes and dislikes. This should have been taken into consideration by their parents.

Jerry: Possibly, as in other character studies we will make, will we note the importance of right choice-making and the tragedy of making the wrong choice as we will learn from Rebekah.

Rick: I have been reminded again, and we can see evidence in the story of the Bible truth, "Be sure your sins will find you out." It's a fact. Every member of Rebekah's family proves this. Isaac was, no doubt, reaping his cowardly act of deception when he lied to the Philistines about Rebekah, his wife.

Bart: Having looked at myself through the characters in this study, I have made up my mind to listen to the passage of Scripture in Galatians 6:6: "Be not deceived; God is not mocked: for whatsoever a man soweth, that shall he also reap." Not only was this true with Rebekah; it was true with Isaac, Esau, and Jacob. It will apply to every one of us.

Chet: Bart's right. Let me add a word to what he said. There are some things that cannot be undone. I know that God forgives us of our sins, but he doesn't stop the results of those sins. When we repent of a wrong choice we have made, he forgives us, but the effect of the choice will run its course. We should always remember that wrong choices, hurtful words, selfish acts, and cunning tricks can be forgiven, but they must run their course. We cannot stop, or change the results.

Candy: Rebekah and Jacob were no less guilty of cheating, robbing, and deceiving, but Esau was receiving the payment of his own sins. Esau forfeited his inheritance when he put his appetite of the moment above the satisfaction of his heart, and traded his birthright to his younger brother for what amounted to beans and rice.

Pastor: It seems providential that, so far, all of your comments have been prompted by the weaknesses, bad traits, and sins of our characters. If we can only profit from the lessons. . . . Has anyone discovered anything good in Rebekah that might be helpful to us?

Sarah: With all of Rebekah's faults, she had a consuming ambition to see her son, Jacob, fulfill the role that God had for him in the life of Israel. Rebekah, of course, remembered that God had said, "The older son will serve the younger." Although she did not understand all God intended, she would do all she could to see it happen as the Lord desired.

Rebekah could detect in Jacob a spiritual discernment—which he showed early in life. The two sons were way apart in spirit and attitude. That's easy to see. Esau seemed to have no concern for the spiritual things of life, but Jacob did. By no means am I defending this mother's schemes or the favoritism she showed, but I do feel that she felt justified in her tactics, because of her consuming passion to see Jacob fulfill God's place in life for him.

Pastor: There's no end to the lessons we can pick up from each of these Bible characters. It's still appropriate—no two wrongs make a right. God doesn't expect wrong choices. He's not pleased with any of us when we make the wrong choice, or have the wrong attitude, or display a spirit of jealousy, partiality, selfish ambition, or perform acts hurtful to another person.

Cheating, robbing, tricks, harmful words or deeds, partiality in the home—all fall into the category of sin. Of such, we must have no part. Any of these will rob you of doing the will of God.

Remember, too, that God has a plan for every life, and he is able to produce and make that life fruitful and happy without our conniving assistance. The things required by the Lord are that you accept his will for your life, die to self daily, let Christ live his life in and through you. Then, you can say with the apostle Paul, "Not I, but Christ who liveth in me" (Gal. 2:20).

SPIRITUAL THERAPY

To get the most personal benefit from this character study, take a pencil and a sheet of paper and answer the following questions.

1. What were the strong points or characteristics of the character? List them on paper.

2. What were the weaknesses of this character? List them.

3. What did the character have going for him or her? List the things in his favor.

4. What decisions or choices did the character make that you think were wrong? List the wrong ones, then list the right ones.

5. How can you benefit by your study of this character?

6. Have you really been face to face with yourself?

Notes:

2
Grapes or Grasshoppers
(Caleb)
Numbers 13:6, 13:17-14:45; Joshua 14:6-15, 15:13-16

Every American boy has his heroes. If you can get into his room, for the equipment and "junk" he collects, on his walls you may see pictures of those he admires most.

I, too, have my heroes. And Caleb, son of Jephunneh from the tribe of Judah, is one of my favorites. Let me share with you how he became one of my heroes.

Not long out of slavery in Egypt, his people had come to a dead standstill on their journey into a great and good land the Lord had promised them. Under their deliverer and leader, Moses, all had gone well on their short journey from Goshen to Kadesh-barnea.

Well, I should not keep you from an incident or two that transpired before Caleb and his company reached this port of embarkation into their new land. Their new land, it should have been.

If God had not stopped Pharaoh and his army, the children of Israel could not have escaped from the banks of the Red Sea. But God stopped Pharaoh dead in his tracks and in the middle of the sea, at that. God had enough of that troublemaker, and I figure he thought that Pharaoh had troubled his favored people too long already.

At least one other problem bothered Moses early on his journey toward the Promised Land. The Bible puts it in these words: "And the mixed multitude that was among them fell a-lusting" (Num. 11:4). Usually, when there is one "gripe" in the bunch, there are others of kindred spirit who join them.

This is what happened. Enough of the crowd—that remembered

the fish, melons, cucumbers, leeks, onions, and garlic of Egypt—complained and griped that the multitude became upset with their status on the journey (Num. 11:5). Seeing that his company was becoming disturbed, Moses became upset. And when that happened, God took over.

The Bible states: "When the people complained it displeased the Lord; and the Lord heard it; and his anger was kindled; and the fire of the Lord burnt among them and consumed them that were in the uttermost parts of the camp." For your benefit, let me tell you where this tragedy took place. You may want to get a map and trace the rest of this journey with the faithful ones who were not destroyed. The place Moses called "Taberah," because it meant the place where the "fire of the Lord" burned among his people.

Stay with me on this journey because there are others in the company who will never make it into the Promised Land. You may be surprised at who they are, and why they didn't make it, even though God had promised it to them.

As in any huge company of people, you will find those of confidence and trust. Let us call this faith in God. This multitude was no exception. After a short stopoff at Mount Sinai for some detailed instructions from the Lord concerning the journey, Moses led the Israelites to Kadesh-barnea, which should have been their place of departure into the fruitful land to which they had started. Canaan was to be their home. It had everything awaiting them.

For fear that there was some "catch" in the whole matter, enough of the people in the crowd balked on their leader, Moses. They wanted to possess the good land, but what if they failed in their attempt?

Some of the strangers in the company started a movement to force the hand of Moses. They demanded that they remain at Kadesh-barnea until a sufficient investigation was made.

They came up with the idea that some spies should survey the land to see if they thought it were possible to take it. This went "against the grain" with their leader, but "God spake unto Moses, saying send thou men that they may search the land of Canaan, which I give unto the children of Israel: of every tribe of their fathers shall ye send a man, everyone a ruler among them."

Here I met Caleb for the first time. It will not be the last, for you are about to be introduced to a man among men. One of my favorite heroes.

In naming the twelve spies, one from each tribe, Moses said, "Of the tribe of Judah, Caleb the son of Jephunneh" (Num. 13:6).

Among the men to spy out the land, you could count on Caleb. He had no idea of searching the good land that the Lord had given to them for obstacles or hindrances: he was not of that stripe. He was an optimist and not a pessimist. He accentuated the positive and eliminated the negative. Never was he numbered with or company to complainers.

These twelve set out on their mission. They were to spend forty days to examine the Promised Land. They went from the wilderness of Zin to Rehob, and thence to Hebron.

The grapes were so fantastic at the Brook of Eschol that the spies could not pass up the opportunity to take their first souvenirs. The cluster of grapes from only one branch was so huge that it required two men to bear it between them on a staff. The pomegranates and the figs were so delicious that they also plucked samples of them.

Truly, the land was one "flowing with milk and honey."

At the end of forty days the twelve spies came marching into camp with their trophies. When they returned to give account of themselves, you would have thought that our Congress was in session. The spies had a majority and a minority report. My hero gave the minority report. What's so good about that? Let's see.

According to the Word of God, the twelve spies were "everyone a ruler among them." Even though the land was goodly, the spies reported that they saw Anakim in the land, giants. Why, the majority report indicated that the Israelities were like grasshoppers in comparison to them! What could mere Israelities do against them? So, they thought they were whipped, and they were.

My hero Caleb thought better of himself than a grasshopper.

The reason: his God was greater than all, and his faith in God gave him a different attitude.

In making its report, the entire committee agreed on one conclusion, namely: "The land is good and great, it is a land flowing with milk and honey as we had been told. We have with us proof to this fact."

But the committee split at this point. The majority, made up of ten, said: "Nevertheless, the people are strong that dwell there in this land. The cities have high walls around them. Moreover, we saw the sons of Anak there. Giants they are, and we are as grasshoppers by their side."

While these rulers of unbelief made their report, urging the people to refuse an attempt at possession of the land, Caleb waited his turn like a gentleman. But no sooner had the majority report been made, my hero came alive. No one better than the Holy Spirit himself could repeat his report and reveal his character. So, let the Bible give his minority report: "And Caleb stilled the people before Moses, and Caleb said, Let us go up at once, and possess it, for we are well able to overcome it" (Num. 13:30).

The debate continued a long time. And even though Joshua, the son of Nun, one of the twelve spies, also took Caleb's side, the ten with the negative report prevailed. The multitude became so upset over the situation, they decided that they would have been better off to have died in Egypt. An attempt was made by the multitude to gather the people and to rally around another leader besides Moses. They would forsake Moses and head back to the land of slavery.

But one thing for sure, whether these children of Israel were conscious of it or not, they had more than Moses to deal with. They were not rebelling against a human leader in Moses; they had sinned against Jehovah God.

God's response was not one that made the whole lot of them happy. God's reaction to the minority report was: "And the Lord said unto Moses . . . how long will it be ere they believe me, for all the signs which I have shewed among them? . . . Because all those men which have seen my glory, and my miracles, which I did in Egypt and in the wilderness, and have tempted me now these ten times, and have not hearkened unto my voice; surely they shall not see the land which I sware unto their fathers, neither shall any of them that provoked me see it. But my servant Caleb, because he had another spirit with him, and hath followed me fully, him will I bring into the land whereinto he went: and his seed shall possess it" (Num. 14:11, 22-24).

The Bible doesn't leave it at that point. It says more–don't miss it.

To his disobedient and unfaithful followers God declared: "Your carcases shall fall in this wilderness; and all that were numbered of you, according to your whole number, from twenty years old and upward, which have murmured against me. Doubtless ye shall not come into the land, concerning which I sware to make you dwell therein, save Caleb the son of Jephunneh, and Joshua the son of Nun" (Num. 14:29-30).

But God was not done speaking at that. He had news, sure enough for those unbelievers. Hear him! "But your little ones, which ye said should be a prey, them will I bring in, and they shall know the land which ye have despised. But as for you, your carcases, they shall fall in this wilderness" (Num. 14:31-32).

For forty years, a year for every day the spies spent in Canaan, the children of Israel wandered in the wilderness. During which time our hero Caleb had to watch die and bury all those over twenty years of age who refused to march into the Promised Land.

While waiting for all those funerals in the wilderness, their children, along with Moses, Joshua, and Caleb had to pay the price of wandering for the forty years bearing the "whoredoms" of their parents until every one of their carcases wasted in the wilderness.

The Bible states further, "And the men, which Moses sent to search the land, who returned, and made the congregation to murmur against him, by bringing up a slander on the land, even those men that did bring up evil report upon the land, died by the plague before the Lord. But Joshua . . . and Caleb, . . . which were of the men that went to search the land, lived still"

(Num. 14:36-38).

It was a forty-year wait for Caleb, but nowhere in the Bible do we find him chafing or complaining over the wilderness wanderings. He had a better spirit than that.

Caleb was forty years older when they marched out of the wilderness than he was when they began this journey. For the next chapter in his life, turn with me to the book of Joshua, chapter 14. The Jordan had been crossed; the good and fruitful land had been entered. The time had come to assign certain portions to the various tribes and their families.

Caleb displays his heroic spirit of unfailing faith, once again. Even until then the sons of Anak, the giants, still possessed Hebron, a valuable portion of the land. Although eighty years old at the time, Caleb asked for the privilege of taking Hebron from the giants, who had forty years before caused some "pygmies" to look upon themselves as grasshoppers.

Having asked for that rugged mountain, the hardest track among them, Caleb went up to possess it. Not in the power and might of Caleb but in his Lord.

The Bible says: "And Caleb drove thence the three sons of Anak, Sheshai, and Ahiman, and Talmai, the children of Anak" (Josh. 15:14).

Hebron, the home of the giants, therefore became the inheritance of Caleb, my hero, because "he wholly followed the Lord God of Israel" (Josh. 14:14).

Of the hundreds of thousands–some say millions–of his day, Caleb is one of four that lives in God's hall of fame. In your generation who do you guess will be remembered? And for what?

SELF-ANALYSIS

Let's do a quick personal examination. How much of you do you see in Caleb? Can you be classified with him, or would you fall into the category of the ones who gave the majority report?

What would you do if you had a giant to face? Would you retreat, or would you face him? Twelve men saw giants; ten of them retreated; two said, "We are well able." God and Moses became "uptight" with these cowards.

If you are not afraid of what you might do, put this aside for a moment. Take a pencil and paper and make a list of the giants in your life. They may be something like these: your purpose in life, your parents, your hero, or your peers. Well, you make your own list. Remember what these can do to you, unless you face them head-on like Caleb did.

The ten spies helped bring back the huge cluster of grapes, yet they allowed giants to get into their eyes and spoil the whole thing for them and for many others.

Caleb would wait, but he would not quit. Defeat wasn't in Caleb's vocabulary. With you, is it grapes or grasshoppers? Remember that in most instances giants must be overcome before we gain the grapes.

Even Gideon said, "The sword of the Lord and of Gideon," so did Caleb. He had no intention of defeating his giants within his own strength. He wholly followed the Lord.

God's hall of fame is made up of the faithful who manifest faith in him. They cannot be swayed by public opinion, the crowd, or other circumstances.

Caleb's humility was due to his dedication to God. His lifetime commitment held him on course. He could not be detoured. His faith held him in line.

It is a pity for God to have to turn to some other to get done what he intended that you or I do.

One closing question: For what do you intend to be remembered? Don't seek to follow Caleb's example without his commitment. "I wholly followed the Lord." What will the record say twenty, forty, sixty years from today concerning you?

If we are grasshoppers in our own eyes, we will never overcome the giants in our lives.

What would you have to change in your life to become a Caleb?

At present, is your attitude more like Caleb's than that of the ten spies who brought in the majority report?

Can you see any of the mixed multitudes attitude in you? Are you on the side of the strangers in the crowd who always complained about their lot?

Will the decisions you make in life, due to your attitude, be hurtful to all those around you, like the decision of the ten spies?

No one but you can determine whether you will be a conqueror, a coward, a giant or a pygmy.

The person you are becoming is the person you are now deciding to be.

Remember the tragic results of the wrong decision made by the crowd. The crowd in this case proved to be dead wrong. It is not always right, nor is it always best to follow the crowd. No doubt Caleb was criticized for his minority stand, yet he was right–God said so.

It may seem tough to stand alone today, but right will ultimately win.

The hero from every crowd will be the one who champions what is right.

NOW, FACE TO FACE WITH YOURSELF

Jed: Let me make a confession. Up until tonight I have attempted to overcome the giants in my life in my own strength. I have known part of the story of Caleb. I knew he overcame the giants in Hebron, but the thing that has impressed me most in this study is that Caleb wholly followed the Lord. I now understand why he could make a minority report and urge the people to go into the land for they were well able. His trust was in the Lord.

I know that I can do a better job putting down the giants that have at times conquered me, for I have turned them over to the Lord. Paul's words, "I can do all things through Christ who strengthens me," have taken on new meaning since studying the life of Caleb.

Janice: I feel somewhat like Jed. So many times I have felt sorry for myself. But since God is the same today, yesterday, and forever I can trust him to help me conquer my giants.

Curtis: I, too, have learned the lessons mentioned by Janice and Jed, but there is another thing that I have made up my mind about during this study. I have determined that God will not ever have to turn to my children or someone else to do what he intended for me to do. The ten spies making the majority report set God's work back forty years. He had to bury all their bodies in the wilderness and wait to grow up a generation that he could use—that would do as Caleb, "wholly follow the Lord."

Nancy: Well, I guess we can conclude that if we are grasshoppers in our own eyes, then we *are* grasshoppers. It's like the old adage: "If you think you can't, then you are right—you can't. But if you think God can, then you are right—you can." Feeling as I do now, I would join sides with Caleb and his minority report, and I request this class to pray for me, that I will always take this stand.

Danny: No doubt all of us will be stronger in the Lord after living with a giant killer such as Caleb during these hours together. But let me remind you, as I have myself, that the Lord makes the difference. With him we can't fail; without him we are a failure already. Remember: "It is not by might, nor by power, but by my spirit, saith the Lord of Hosts." Like Caleb, our success must be in the power of the Lord.

SPIRITUAL THERAPY

To get the most personal benefit from this character study, take a pencil and a sheet of paper and answer the following questions.

1. What were the strong points or characteristics of the character? List them on paper.

2. What were the weaknesses of this character? List them.

3. What did the character have going for him or her? List the things in his favor.

4. What decisions or choices did the character make that you think were wrong? List the wrong ones, then list the right ones.

5. How can you benefit by your study of this character?

6. Have you really been face to face with yourself?

Notes:

3
The Champion of Israel
(Samson)
Judges 13-16; Hebrews 11:32,39

The story you are about to read is true. And the name has not been changed to protect the guilty. Most of his lifestory is found in the book of Judges, chapters 13-16. But please do not give up on him and cast him aside without reading the account in Hebrews 11:32, 39 where God reserved in heaven a place for him alongside Abraham, Moses, Gideon, Barak, David, and Samuel.

Don't for one minute conclude that his story is recorded in the Bible because of his strength. Neither should you assume that it is there for fascinating entertainment. Everyone who knew him recognized he could rip a lion's jaw apart single-fisted, but this is not the reason his story is told in the Holy Bible. Those left to tell the story knew about his strength to pull down the temple of Dagon and kill hundreds of people. But the Bible had a better reason for telling his story. Samson's story is written in the Bible to explain how a loving God forgives sinners and gives them another chance when they repent and seek it, whether they fulfill all of his purpose or not. True, the story would have been better had he completely done God's will.

There was political unrest in his country. More than 300 years had passed since Moses, the lawgiver, had disappeared and was considered dead.

The Philistines were a constant threat to his people. Their lands joined, and they had invaded and taken possession of a strip of the territory that was next to them. What more they would take next, only they knew. This never ceased to be a problem to Samson's people.

One day an angel of Jehovah appeared to one of the most devout and God-fearing couples among God's chosen people. He promised them a son who would begin to deliver Israel from the oppression of the Philistines (Judg. 13:5). This was indeed good news to people who had been overrun so many times by this enemy.

The angel gave detailed instructions to the parents concerning their son who was to begin delivering their people from the dreadful oppressor.

In keeping with the angel's promise, a baby boy was born. His parents, though quite elderly, began to school him as soon as he could understand the angel's instructions. Realizing early in life why God had brought him into the world, he desired to follow his instructions as carefully as possible. He observed the diet. No one was allowed to cut his hair.

Although regrettable things happened in his life, and he did many things about which he never was proud, his heart's intention was to please God with his life. The desire of Samson was to do God's will. All must agree that his life really was a mixture of good and evil. No matter how many times it happened, he never could be happy with himself when he disobeyed God. When he sought God's forgiveness, he gave it.

As he grew up, Samson's physique angered friends and neighbors. To serve God in the capacity for which he was brought into the world, he had to have a strong, healthy body. So, he developed muscles. While growing up, even in his teens, he was the ideal of all the kids, especially the girls, for he was the athlete type, par excellence.

Having such wonderful opportunity, being the idol of all the girls, finally led to his downfall. Although strong in so many respects, he through weakness fell for a heathen girl, when he could have had the girl of his choice—one of his own people possessing the same faith. Instead he let Satan entangle him with a Philistine girl.

This seriously upset his parents who felt responsible to God for his disobedience. Severely, they warned him of what God, through Moses, had said concerning marriage outside of their faith (Deut. 7:1-3).

Love is a strange thing. Try as hard as he could, it was impossible for Samson to stay away from his new friend, even though she was one of the enemies of his people.

A strange thing happened on one of his trips to visit his girl friend. While crossing a vineyard on his way, a roaring lion made an approach at him. Not realizing his strength, but with no other choice—for the lion was in midair on his way to devour him—he tackled him single-handedly.

Having no other weapon, with his bare hands Samson killed that lion. Never before had Samson felt the Spirit of the Lord come upon him in such force. Realizing this to be true, he gave God the glory, but he went on to see his girl friend, anyway (Judg. 14:6).

From all that his parents had taught him about their conversation with the angel of the Lord, Samson knew God had something in store for him, but he had no idea of what it was.

Feeling that he was developing into a super-strong man, his ambition began to get the best of him. But as he looked back over the situation, he could see that, while he was about to destroy himself by disobedience to God's will, God rescued him. He had a purpose for Samson's life. God used every available means to encourage Samson to do that.

In his disobedience, God never gave him up. He had a job for him to do and though God put handicaps and obstacles in his path, he always left the decision for Samson to make. God doesn't force anyone to do his will.

All too often, Samson showed no gratitude to God for coming mightily upon him and making his deliverance possible. At times he almost thought it was due to his own strength.

As he passed the carcass of the dead lion, Samson saw a swarm of bees about the skull. To his discovery, the skull of the carcass was filled with delicious honey, a part of which he ate on his way home, and he shared some with his parents.

Although his parents resented his courtship with the heathen girl, he kept courting their favor. You see, when a Hebrew was a young person, his parents arranged the weddings for him. So, he had to have their consent before he could be married.

At last his parents gave in and the wedding was arranged—even though they were not too highly pleased. For they felt sure that it was not in the will of God. At least they didn't think it could be.

As was the custom, a long reception followed the wedding. It was also very common for the groomsmen to demand a riddle from the groom. It always cost either the groom or the groomsmen because if they could not guess the riddle put forth by the groom, they had to present him with presents. If they guessed it, the groom paid off.

Samson was set with a riddle. He felt certain that it could never be guessed. When the occasion came, he told his riddle. It was this: "Out of the eater came something to eat, out of the strong came something sweet" (Judg. 14:14). If either of the thirty groomsmen guessed the riddle, he was to give each of them two suits of clothing. If they failed, each one of them would give him two suits. Not even his parents knew where the honey came from, so he felt perfectly safe.

One day passed. They guessed and guessed but, never the answer. The third day came and the groomsmen, all Philistines, became anxious and even fearful of not answering his riddle. They hadn't even come close to the solution.

Among his groomsmen were those who bargained with his bride to find the answer to his riddle. When she swore to them that she didn't know the answer, they threatened her life. This ruined his honeymoon, and his bride wept the other four days of the wedding feast.

Finally, to stop the flow of her tears and to go on with the honeymoon, Samson gave in and confided with her the riddle. As soon as he told her the answer, she rushed to the groomsmen with the solution to save her own life.

The honeymoon, almost over, at which time the riddle must

be solved, a groomsman approached him with the answer. When he asked him, "What is sweeter than honey? What is stronger than a lion?" Samson knew what had happened.

For the first time in his life, he had been double-crossed. He couldn't take it. And, too, strong man that he was, he decided to get revenge. Even though he had been betrayed by his wife, he would keep his promise and give each man his two suits. But before he did that, he stormed at the traitors, "If you had not plowed with my heifer, you would not have found my riddle."

How the Lord ever forgave Samson is grace, for in a fury, he killed the first thirty Philistine men he found. He took their clothes and threw them down at the feet of his betrayers and went home to his parents, leaving his "heifer" behind.

Their marriage lasted only through the honeymoon, and much of that was unhappy. This should have been lesson enough to put him into God's will. But sad to say, his blunders had just begun.

After about three months, he decided to go back to his Philistine wife. Upon his arrival at the home of her parents, he learned that she had married the best man in his wedding. Well, this he just wouldn't take lying down. The "self" in him came alive. He would make somebody pay dearly for this. In a fit of temper, he went out and caught 300 foxes, paired them off in twos, tied their tails together with a firebrand to each, and sent those wild, screaming animals across the ripe, ready to harvest, grainfields of the Philistines. The wind was up that day and, brother, did that fire clean out the Philistines!

Poor girl! She had as well died at the hands of his groomsmen, because—when those farmers heard that he had burned their harvest because his wife had married his best man—they killed her entire family (Judg. 15:6).

By this time the Philistines had concluded that they couldn't handle him and, too, his people were wondering what they were going to do with him. At the request of Samson's people who had agreed that they would help the Philistines capture him, he agreed to let them tie him with ropes if they would not harm him.

They agreed. He came down from the top of the hill to let them bind him. Not far away, the Philistine army stood watch, ready to rush upon him when his people had him sufficiently bound. After they had him bound, his people fled from the scene. As never before, he knew that without the help of God, he was a "goner"—because the Philistines would soon rush upon him. But just in the nick of time the Spirit of God came mightily upon him. The only weapon at hand was the jawbone of a dead donkey. He grabbed it up and one by one, as those Philistines came at Samson they lay dead in their tracks. Pile after pile of men lay dead. He had to move about from one place to another for the dead men to have a place to fall.

After the fierce battle was over and he viewed the situation, Samson said: "Heaps upon heaps I have slain a thousand men" (Judg. 15:16).

Little did he know it but in all his disobedience and rebellion against God, God was using Samson to "begin to deliver Israel from the Philistines."

Evidently there were better ways to deliver his people, for seemingly, he was doing it the hard way. But it was amazing to have the Spirit of God come mightily upon him just in time, at the right time, to win the victory.

By this time he had the enemy on the run. His parents had decided perhaps the Lord had something to do with his marriage into the Philistine camp. It put Samson in better position for God to use him to bring harm to his enemies.

Not more than five or six miles from Zorah was the city of Timnah, which actually was a city of Judah that was at the time occupied by the enemy. And because he had caused so much trouble in Timnah that the Philistines had killed his wife and her father, he decided to spend some time in Gaza. This was an exciting trade center just off the coast of the great sea. And, too, it was on the main highway that led up from Egypt.

Samson did not share with us all that happened to him that night in Gaza. For one thing, he let a new girl friend keep him inside the city wall until the night guard had locked the gate to the city, so that one could neither enter nor leave through the balance of the night. Upon his arrival at the gate, the keeper refused to unlock it, because it was midnight and the gate was not to be opened after that time. Usually, one way or another getting what he wanted, Samson didn't argue much with the night watchman. But when he deliberately refused to open the gate, Samson became enraged. So Samson reached for the gate which was supported by posts securely fastened in the ground. Never ceasing to be astonished and amazed at how the Spirit of the Lord came mightily upon him upon such occasions, he lifted the gate, posts and all, and walked off up the hill with the entire works. He carried the thing almost to Hebron, which was about forty miles away.

His father, Manoah, had died, but his mother was at home ill at the time. Thus, from Hebron he started home to Zorah. His quenchless love for the woman he had courted until midnight in Gaza had Samson all set to make her a return visit. After telling his mother about his new girl, Delilah, he left home for the Sorek river valley to see his lover again.

Although he dearly loved Delilah, he found out the hard way that she never did love him. She finally pulled "a fast one" on him. But he had it coming to him.

The Philistine government bought over his girl friend. They sent messengers to Delilah to offer her bribes if she would reveal the secret to Samson's strength. This time the approach was different from the one they used on his wife in Timnah. They threatened her life and that of her father. Great sums of money were offered Delilah. At first she refused. They raised the amount of the bribe—five hundred pieces of silver, a thousand, two thousand. When Delilah insisted that she would not reveal the secret to his strength, they made her an offer that she could not refuse. The five Philistine lords each flashed 1,100 pieces of silver at her—a total of 5,500 pieces of silver. The girl could resist the temptation no longer. Delilah yielded.

Not knowing about the contract that his lover had with his enemies, Samson fell into her trap. Delilah was a charming girl.

Not only did he fall for her beauty and charm, he let her cunning devices lead to his downfall. She tried several ways to seduce the truth of his strength from him, but each time he got her off his back.

Delilah stopped nothing short of doing her best to deceive Samson. To her, it was nothing to prepare him a delicious meal, then lull him to sleep in her arms and on her lap. With this sort of thing the wicked woman got to her man.

Three times Samson had deceived her and she had called for the men to bring the bribe and she was embarrassed to see the officials take away the 5,500 pieces of silver. Delilah was desperate. No doubt she had planned how she would spend and enjoy the bribe money but so far she had failed to find what was behind the strong man's strength.

In her desperation to discover his secret, and having tried every other thing she could devise, Delilah broke into tears. She wept and wept. Not able to stand those tears, finally, he told her his heart. He had taken a vow to God (Num. 6:18). His long hair indicated Samson's dependance upon God.

Soon after he had revealed to Delilah the secret to his strength, she got busy. Before he knew it, she had lulled him to sleep on her knees and the tough boys not only brought along the bribe money, they had a barber with them. Though foolish man that he was, while trusting a woman he loved, asleep on her lap Samson's beautiful locks were cut off. When he arose to shake himself and exert his power, the poor fellow had none. The Lord had departed with his strength and there he was, helpless. With only his ordinary strength he was quickly subdued. Not taking any chances, those tough guys gouged out Samson's eyes. They tore them out by the roots. After that he was taken to Gaza as their prisoner.

Thinking his strange power might return, those soldiers bound him with extra heavy, strong bronze fetters.

When the Philistines knew that their worst enemy was captured, that he could no longer see, and that he was sufficiently bound, they had a ball. For twenty years they had lived in fear of this strong man. Now that he was helpless, they must celebrate. Celebrate, they did.

Festivities were planned. People flocked into the city to enjoy the sights and the fun. And, too, some of them were ready to give credit to their god, Dagon. The major festivities were held in the temple built to his honor.

During his stay in the Philistine prison, his hair grew again. Knowing why God allowed his shame and disgrace, Samson made it right with God again. Everytime he disobeyed, God forgave him when he sought forgiveness. Even though God forgave Samson for his sin with the girl in the Valley of Sorek, the results of his sins could not be stopped. So he lingered in prison and from day to day they hitched him, instead of a donkey, to the mill and used him to grind the grain.

At last, the day of celebration had come for the Philistines to toast the downfall of Israel's champion. The people had gathered from everywhere around. Three thousand of them had climbed to the roof of the temple to observe the spectacle, their former menace, Samson. Once again he was to be in the limelight, but this time he was the circus. It was to be so different from the times when he had been the champion of the occasion. This was to disgrace God's cause, thought the Philistines.

To the shame and disgrace of himself, his family, his people, and to the dishonor of God, with his eyes gouged out, the once consecrated man made sport for the enemy. Blinded, grinding yet bound, he was made a spectacle to what sin will do.

As he entered the stage, the crowd exploded with jeers of derision. They cried: "Great is Dagon, the god of the Philistines." This broke Samson's heart, but when the same jeering crowd cried out, "Down with Jehovah, Samson's God and the God of Israel," it was too much for the once-successful man.

Such humiliation, disgrace, and shame had never before come to the cause of Jehovah and it was all his fault. He had caused it.

To add to the humiliation of "The Strong Samson," an innocent little boy had been assigned the task of leading him around on the stage.

Having troubled the Philistines for twenty years, Samson knew something about the temple erected to their god, Dagon. Although he was blind, he remembered how the people boasted about the main weight of the entire upper structure of the temple being supported by two pillars near the stage. Having repented for his sin, he had received forgiveness from the Lord. Even though his shame had to take its course, Samson began to pray that for one more time God would get glory unto Himself through him. If only God would allow him the strength to pull those two pillars out of their sockets, once and for all time the heathen god, Dagon, would be disgraced and dethroned in the minds of his followers. Then Jehovah would receive the glory.

Once again he began to feel the presence of Jehovah. Was he going to be given one other chance? He prayed as he had never prayed. Samson's faith began to become stronger and the little boy who had the leash to which he was tied seemed very nice and friendly. He played into Jehovah's hands also.

Expressing to the lad his tired feelings, he whispered to him a request. He let him rest for a moment against the two pillars that supported the upper structure of the temple. When the Philistines decided that their victim was physically exhausted, they came alive with shouts of joy that the twenty-year champion was so weak and tired that he had to lean on the pillars for rest.

With his head bowed, the crowd thinking that he was resting, Samson lifted his voice up to heaven. He prayed for God to give him one more chance. He did. Samson felt him like that before, and he knew that God had heard a sinner's plea. God was willing to give him another chance to glorify him.

His muscles bulged and strained. Perspiration beaded on Samson's forehead like drops of blood. He heard one pillar crash, then the other. They buckled, then started crumbling. They fell apart. The roof, along with the three thousand Philistines that had perched on it, came tumbling in on him and the rest of the crowd. Samson was slain with the host of the Philistines. But Samson knew that in his death God accomplished more to free his people than he did through his life (Judg. 16:23-32).

CHARACTER ANALYSIS

It seems strange that Samson would think he could judge Israel when he could not handle himself. If he had remained committed to God, the Philistines could never have taken him captive.

Samson is a good example of a once-consecrated man who "blew" it. He should be a lesson to us that the consecrated person has God on his side. Nothing seemed impossible as long as Samson was in God's will.

Another truth we should learn from Samson is that the consecrated person is always in danger of the snares of the devil. Satan always has a barber ready to give a hair cut in the devil's barbershop.

Like he did with Samson, the devil makes a big to-do over our successes. It is at this point that with a proud, haughty spirit a person falls into Satan's trap. Pride has led to the downfall of more people than most other sins.

If it is possible for a person to profit by the mistakes of another, surely we can profit by the disgrace that came to a once-consecrated person. With his eyes gouged out, his beautiful locks shaved off, bound with chains of brass, grinding at the mill, Samson is an example of what sin will do for a person, even though at one time he had enjoyed the blessings and power of God upon his life.

Our character learned the hard way that his strength was not within himself; it came from God. This once physical giant became a moral pygmy. What a pity! A man with the physical strength to carry away the gate of a city, yet without enough moral strength to resist a harlot in the valley of Sorek.

Danger lurks in bad company. It harbors in high places. Let a good person begin to play loose in the wrong place with the wrong people and his locks begin to fall.

That alcoholic didn't intend to go that far when he took the first drink. That beautiful girl didn't plan to become a prostitute when she began to take liberties with her body.

God uses men with many faults—sometimes serious faults. God's use of faulty people in no wise condones weakness and error.

Even though Samson was foolish enough to reveal the secret of his strength to Delilah, God employed him to win many victories over the Philistines.

Unlimited resources and power were Samson's, if only he had added wisdom and loyalty to his strength and courage. Courage and strength without wisdom cause trouble. Under extremely serious conditions God used the best man available in Samson.

Samson is an example of God's power when he can find a faithful champion for his cause. At his best, Samson is an example of the power of a consecrated man. He is an example of what a person can do when he is in God's will.

Samson is an example of the disgrace of a once dedicated man. He is an example of a man who wants another chance. He is a testimony to what God can do even with what is left of a person, no matter what his condition, if he repents and seeks to do the will of God. When in the will of God, Samson championed Israel's cause without fail.

Samson is a typical example of the danger that faces every Christian who allows temptation to overcome him. Samson should teach us to stay away from the wrong company. There is danger in evil companions. He also should teach us to fear our weaknesses and go strong on dependence upon God.

God always gave Samson enough strength to do the task He assigned him. Although he was committed to God's will, there were still human and sinful tendencies present with him.

This physically strong man was never pleased with himself. When in a fit of temper, he lost control of himself and disobeyed God. Samson's disobedience always led to repentance. Sin and disobedience can be forgiven, but the results will reap the harvest. God's abounding love for sinners is ready to forgive and restore.

Samson found that God is ready to give a second chance. Even though a second chance is possible, it can never be what the first chance should have been. Sometimes God takes our mistakes and uses them for good.

There is no God but Jehovah God and it is tragic folly to worship idols. Those that misplace their trust will find one day that their idols will fail them. The servants of the Lord are always in danger of their locks being shorn in the devil's barbershop.

The Bible is as free to record the sins of God's people as it is to record the good that they did.

It is not good for different faiths to be linked up in marriage. Samson had a lustful desire and weakness for strange women. A house divided against itself cannot stand. And Samson fell into the trap and went down because of it. The company one keeps makes or breaks him.

God has a plan for every life. To stay in his will and plan for your life is the determining factor of a happy and helpful life, or the downfall of it.

God is going to have his will and way done in some lives—others he has to wait for someone else to fulfill his purpose. Therefore, it is sound judgment to join up with God, and let him steer your course. Then you will come out victorious.

It was not due to Samson's success, failure, sin, or goodness that God gave him a place alongside of Abraham, Moses, Barak, and others. It was due to his faith in and the faithfulness of a true and loving God.

PERSONAL OBSERVATIONS

Larry: "Birds of a feather flock together." That proved true in Samson's case. It may have exceptions, but society fails to recognize them.

Paul: Larry has gone right to the heart of it. It's bad that Samson couldn't live consistently for God. Shakespeare said something about: "Defend your reputation, or bid farewell to your good life forever."

Tracy: That reminds me of the Bible verse which says, "A good name is more precious than ointment, and is rather to be chosen than great riches."

Sally: Well, one thing for certain, we should learn from this study that we become part of what we read, see, and the people we associate with. We need to be on guard and keep up our defenses. Our lives spill over on others—we are responsible to God for our influence.

Harold: Samson was a strong man, much stronger than some of us, and temptation got him. It's just the truth—we have to be careful of our associates.

Debbie: All that's been said is very helpful, and I am for it, but let me say a word about the other side of the company we keep. There are Christian people that you are around, and they make life better. These are the people you regret to have leave you. With them, you feel good vibrations in your heart.

Pastor: Elizabeth Barrett Browning wrote of such a character as you mentioned.

"She never found fault with you, never implied
Your wrong by her right; and yet men at her side
Grew nobler, girls purer, as through the whole
town
The children were gladder that pulled at her
gown—
My Kate.

"None knelt at her feet confessed lovers in thrall;
They knelt more to God than they used—that
was all;
If you praised her as charming, some asked what
you meant,
But the charm of her presence was felt when she
went—
My Kate."

As Mrs. McKay and I read our Bible reading for the day, the Scripture passage pressed home again the importance of choosing right companions. Let me share two of the verses. As Paul made his urgent appeal to the Christians at Thessalonica: "In the name of our Lord Jesus Christ, that ye withdraw yourselves from every brother that walketh disorderly . . . and have no company with him" (2 Thess. 3:6, 14).

Therefore, realizing that companionship is indispensable, be sure you choose your friends wisely, thoughtfully, and prayerfully. The fulfillment of all the possibilities in you, the unfolding of your resources, the life of your souls therefore depend much on your companions. The best are found in church. And never forget, even though you select and walk with the redeemed of the Lord, you can only complete your spiritual development by walking personally with the Lord himself.

Now would we all agree with the Bible injunction: "The way of the transgressor is hard"?

Not only does the Bible bear this out—secular literature does the same. Listen to Dr. Moore's description in his book, *The Life of Lord Byron:*

"Though gay companions o'er the bowl
Dispel awhile the sense of ill,
Though pleasures fill the maddening soul,
The heart—the heart is lonely still.
Aye, but to die, and go, alas!
Where all have gone and all must go;
To be nothing that I was
Ere born to life and living woe."

In commenting on the life of Lord Byron, James Alexander said: "Byron seemed to have experienced little less than hell upon earth. He was a living example of tormenting powers of uncontrolled selfishness. Remorse without repentance and self-contempt without amendment are dreadful scourges. From country to country he fled but he took the scorpions with him."

To get the most personal benefit from this character study, take a pencil and a sheet of paper and answer the following questions.

1. What were the strong points or characteristics of the character? List them on paper.

2. What were the weaknesses of this character? List them.

3. What did the character have going for him or her? List the things in his favor.

4. What decisions or choices did the character make that you think were wrong? List the wrong ones, then list the right ones.

5. How can you benefit by your study of this character?

6. Have you really been face to face with yourself?

Notes:

4
A Man Who "Blew It"
(Saul)
1 Samuel 9:1-31:13

In desperation, after three hard days in search of his father's donkeys, Saul had decided to consult a seer who lived in Ramah. He was in hopes that he could help him locate the animals. He and his father's servant who were on the search for them had scoured the high country of Ephraim, but with no success. In addition to this, they had scouted the entire territory of Benjamin and had not found the donkeys. The lad just couldn't return home to his father without the herd. Feeling that perhaps the prophet could help, Saul decided to give him a try.

It had not crossed his mind that, while he was searching for the donkeys, the prophet, whom he was about to approach, was looking for a king, at the request of his heavenly Father, Jehovah. Had he known this to be true, it surely would not have occurred to Saul that he may be looking for him.

As Saul approached the prophet, the Lord by some means revealed that Saul was to be the king. Understanding his predicament and his responsibility to his father to locate the animals, Samuel relieved young Saul's mind about the lost donkey. How he knew, Saul didn't know, but Samuel told him that he could forget the donkeys—they had been found.

To Saul's amazement the prophet had previously arranged a banquet in Saul's honor, to which he had gathered thirty guests. Understanding what was taking place and how it had come about, the prospective king was confounded. Even though his father, Kish, was a very wealthy man, with a large farm, he belonged to an insignificant tribe in comparison to some of the rest. The tribe of Benjamin had very little influence or power at that time.

Saul could never forget that banquet. They had arranged for him to sit at the head of the table and he was given the choicest of foods. The prophet, Samuel, informed Saul in the presence of the thirty other guests that he would be anointed king over all the people the next day.

Being head and shoulders taller than any other person, Saul thought, was the reason why he had been chosen. But surely a king, to rule over all God's people, would not be chosen on the basis of his physical appearance. There must be a better reason. Having failed to locate a herd of his father's asses in three hard days, how could he rule his people?

The prophet shared many insights with Saul the next morning, at which time he anointed him as the new king and invoked Jehovah's blessings upon him.

Before leaving him, Samuel foretold several things that would happen to Saul on his way home. Of the events that he said would take place, one was that he would meet some men going to Bethel. Those men would give him two loaves of bread.

It happened just as the prophet had said that it would. Furthermore, when his men saw the mass of the army that they were up against, they fled. They hid in every nook and cranny they could find. Most of Saul's men even crossed the Jordan into the land of Gad. Saul was determined to remain in Gilgal, no matter what happened. Shaking in his boots along with the few of his men who remained with him, he prayed that the prophet would come to his defense. Saul knew that if the prophet would come and offer up to Jehovah a sacrifice that he could handle the situation.

Seven days went by and Samuel didn't show. Saul was having a difficult time trying to keep the few soldiers he had left from deserting. Realizing how nervous he was and how scared his few men were. Saul had to do something. Thus, he took into his own hands the sacred act of offering the sacrifice to Jehovah. This was his first mistake. Just as he had finished this unwise performance, Saul saw Samuel coming. To say the least, the prophet of the Lord was horrified, for he knew that the king had no right to take upon himself such a priestly duty.

When Samuel finished his tonguelashing for that act, Saul realized how sinful he had been. And Because of Saul's sin, the prophet warned him that God would replace him as king. Upon doing this, the prophet started his long journey back to Gibeah.

Were it not for the faith in God that his son, Jonathan, had, and with only six hundred soldiers left who were willing to fight, he would have given up in defeat. Through the heroic efforts of Jonathan and the will of the Lord, they battled the Philistines to their defeat.

This, of course, gave Saul new courage to win further victories over the enemy. When the traitors among his men saw that the victory was won, they began joining in on his side again. Those who had fled to the caves and dens also came out and joined him in the battle.

After Jonathan had led him to victory, Saul consulted the Lord about what to do with the remaining Philistines. At the request of Samuel, he went against the Amalekites for a tremendous victory. But once again he made a terrible mistake. He sinned against the Lord. When the prophet directed him to fight the Amalekites, he ordered him to destroy all of them, their king and all their possessions. Instead of obeying the command, Saul captured Agag, the king, and he kept all of their best animals.

Because of Saul's disobedience, Jehovah sent Samuel back to remind Saul that he was not worthy to be king of his people.

Disappointed with the man he had anointed king of his people, Samuel climbed the arduous road up from the Jordan valley never to lay eyes upon Saul again.

Not only had he disappointed Samuel, Saul had disobeyed God

Why he lied to the prophet of God about the sheep and oxen, I will never understand. It surely got Saul when he heard the bleating of the sheep and lowing of the cattle. Man, did he faint when the man of God looked straight into his eyes and asked, "What meaneth the bleating of the sheep and the lowing of the oxen that I hear?" Saul had "blown it," for sure.

After that Saul no longer took any interest in any of the activities that he had before. He just sat around looking at the walls. People were concerned about him, so they recommended David, a young musician, to lift his spirits by his musical ability. That temporarily helped. For awhile, the young man was such a relief to him that Saul loved him as if he were his own son. David was such a comfort to him that Saul made him his armorbearer, so he could have him around all the time. But one day, as Saul was returning from a battle with the Philistines, some women came out and sang about how David killed 10,000 and that the king had only killed 1,000. This bothered him to no end when he heard about it. The more he thought about it, the madder Saul got. To think that just a boy could win over the hearts of his people and that they would think more of a boy than they would of the king, the one anointed by God. Saul decided to keep an eye on David so that he wouldn't cause trouble. The whole situation kept eating at him until Saul could no longer take it. He had to do something–it was beginning to drive him crazy. Saul thought he had come up with the solution. He sent David out to command 100 men. Saul thought that if the people didn't see him, then they would forget about him, and all his problems would be over. But he was wrong. Every time David went into battle, his fame spread until all the people knew about what a good soldier he was. Saul actually thought that the whole problem was over when he left, but with his victories the problem was there–and even to a greater extent. The more he thought about how popular David had become, the madder Saul got.

Saul knew that he had to do something, but he didn't know what. He even tried to plot to get David killed in battle, but even that failed. He felt like throwing himself off a cliff because nothing was going right. To top the problem off, David doubled the 100 fore-skins of the Philistines he had asked for a dowry for Saul's daughter and then he took her for a wife.

Not only was David a threat to the kingdom, he was also his son-in-law. That put the "icing on the cake."

With each victory, David brought more hatred to Saul's heart.

He even became so mad that he threw a spear at David as he played his harp. Even that didn't work, because that day his aim must have been off beam—he missed him; and his daughter helped David escape. Now, even his own blood had turned on him.

Saul became obsessed with killing David. He had to find some way to get rid of him before David got rid of him. He tried to turn the tribe of Benjamites against him. But the loyal followers that David had, knew that the stories Saul told against David were pure lies.

Finally Saul seized the opportunity. Doeg, the Edomite herdsman, told him that David had stopped at Nob and was taken care of by the priests there. Saul called Ahimelech and his priests before him to see if the story were true about David's being there. Ahimelech vowed his loyalty, but Saul didn't believe him. He ordered his assistants to kill them. But Doeg had no hesitation and before Saul's eyes, he killed eighty-five priests. Saul didn't stop there—he sent Doeg to Nob to destroy all the property that the priests had left behind.

There were other close calls when Saul almost killed David. One was at the city, Keilah, because David had rescued it from the Philistines. But when Saul arrived there, David had already fled, because the people were going to turn him over to Saul.

The other time was when the people of Ziph sent word to Saul that David was in the area. But again the plan fell through, and he got away.

But the time Saul remembered best was when he was coming back from battle with the Philistines and was told that David was in the wilderness of Engedi. Saul commanded 3,000 men in after him. Saul went into a cave to take a rest—of all people, there was David with 600 other men. Saul thought that he'd "had it" after what he'd tried to do to David. David, though, said that Saul was his master, and he wouldn't harm him. Saul was touched by David's loyalty to him and he knew he had done this young man a grave injustice. Saul broke down and in essence told him, "David, you are truly my son, and the kingdom will be in your hands."

Later, suspicious Saul began to have second thoughts. "Did David spare me at the cave only because I had more troops outside?" Saul thought. Now Saul had let David off the hook. David was still running away, and Saul was trying to protect his kingdom. Once again Saul decided that he had better kill David, for fear that David would kill him. The chase was on, but David fled to the land of the Philistines.

Well, at least Saul had David out of his hair. But the Philistines took advantage of Saul's preoccupation with David, and they moved in on his territory. They massed their army to the plain of Esdraelon, where it joins the valley of Jezreel. Saul prepared his army and led it to Mount Gilboa.

It was then that Saul realized that there was neither prophet nor priest to consult. What would he do to attack those Philistines? The only priests left were with David. They took the oracles with them when they fled for their lives.

Saul finally decided that the only recourse was for him to consult a "witch" or medium to give him understanding. So, by night he disguised himself and set out to visit the medium.

When he arrived, he asked if he might speak with the departed spirit of Samuel. To his surprise, and more to the surprise of the medium, Samuel was sent to speak to Saul. Samuel told Saul that he would be defeated and that he and his sons would be killed.

In sheer terror, Saul fell to the floor and wouldn't move. He had to be helped up off of the floor. After eating some food that the medium prepared for him, he started back to the camp. That was the longest 12 miles Saul had ever traveled. All he could think about was what Samuel had related to him and that only tomorrow his life would be over. No doubt all of his deeds, words, and thoughts came through his mind and he began to cry. He knew that he had not only failed God, who had put him on the throne, but also the people that were under his care. Oh, how much better a king Saul could have been if only he had let God control him rather than trying to rule in his own power!

Just like Samuel said, the next day Saul's army went down in defeat. He saw his sons, Jonathan, Abinadab, and Melchishua killed before his own eyes. When the Philistines turned to kill him, rather than let them do it, Saul killed himself on his own sword, along with his armor bearer.

The next day they found his body and those of his sons and they chopped off their heads and hung their bodies on the wall of Beth-shan. Some of his loyal soldiers came at night, took them to Jabech and buried them under the tamaisk trees there.

OBSERVATIONS

As you look back on his life do you see the roads that Saul should have traveled but didn't? How much different could it have been if Saul had listened more closely to Samuel and the priests who tried to guide him in the right direction that God wanted him to go!

We see both good and bad about his life. The kingdom of Israel was united for the only time in history, and there was no major conflict between the 12 tribes. The government was set up fairly well so that all the tribes were treated equally. It was established to meet the needs of the people, whatever they were. Even though Saul was king, he was not far above the common people. They felt like coming to him and talking things over. He even lived in less splendor than all the other kings, because he wanted to be close to the people he loved.

The bad seems to outweigh the good. The jealousy that Saul had for David almost destroyed the kingdom. He didn't take the time to tend to the affairs of his people. He was too far off from reality to know what was happening to his nation.

Saul almost destroyed their religion when he killed the 85 priests. He was raised in a religious home and knew the value it had in the lives of all the people, but he went against what he knew was right and turned his back on God. Saddest of all, God turned his back on Saul. There was no way for him to succeed with God against him. The end had to be like it was because, instead of being a guide, Saul actually stood in the way of God and his Chosen People. We can't know the heartbreak that Saul had when he knew he was to die. Reality came to him and he saw what he had done in 20 years of leading the people that he loved. All the bad things that he did, he had to suffer guilt for. After Saul's story, maybe you won't let anyone put distance between you and God—because the result is the same, death.

Remember, don't ever take the chance on winning a flock of sheep and losing a kingdom. Such happened to Saul.

CHARACTER ANALYSIS

In the days of his strength and wisdom Saul had despised frauds such as witches (as the one of Endor) and all schemes of those who propose to peddle the secrets of God at so much apiece. So much did he despise them, that early in his reign, he had them driven out of the land.

For Saul to finally sink so low and to such a debased position in life that he would call upon a witch was a confession of his complete overthrow in character.

As you read his downfall, remember that it came by his own choice. By his own sin and stubbornness, in disobedience to God, Saul charted his own course. Remember, too, no person ever had a brighter start or a fairer opportunity to succeed than Saul.

Many persons have succeeded in life who didn't have nearly so much going for them. Rather than let circumstances make or break them, they altered the circumstances. To do this, one must plan in advance.

What happened to this man who "blew it" doesn't have to happen to anyone. Saul brought the tragedy upon himself.

The final judgment pronounced by the prophet upon Saul should be a lesson to all who read his story. Memorize these sad words: "Because thou hast rejected the Word of the Lord, he hath rejected thee from being king."

It was too late after the sentence was passed for Saul to hang onto the skirt of the prophet's mantle. The die had been cast. The man who could have been, had sinned away his days of grace.

As the Bible plainly says, "My Spirit will not always strive with man," the words had come true. Another stubborn, disobedient, self-centered person was left to pursue his own wicked course.

Imagine, if you will, a person with everything in his favor, but without regard to his Maker, taking things into his own hands, ignoring the God who chose him and would have blessed him, going his own willful way.

Troubled by an evil spirit, young David was summoned to console the gloomy, melancholy king with his sweet music. But there is nothing in earthly music, no matter how charming, that can permanently silence the accusing conscience in the heart of one with unforgiven sin staring him in the face.

Let us learn one lesson from Saul if nothing else; God refuses to be used as a convenience for men. At heart, Saul was still a mad man, intoxicated with power. He never came before the Lord with a broken and contrite heart. Had he only confessed sincerely and repented for his wrongdoings, forgiveness would have been his immediately. This he didn't do. Had sin not made a fool of the once charming Saul, never would he have entertained the idea that he could force God's hand.

Saul should be a warning to us to seek and do God's will when and while the opportunities come, for to fail to do so is to have the door to such blessings closed in our faces.

Just as it was impossible for Saul to thwart God and approach him some way other than repentance for his sin, the same is true today. God never leaves a person until that person first has left God.

It is impossible for one who has been redeemed by the blood of Jesus Christ to lose his relationship or position as a child of God. It is, however, possible for a disobedient child to waste his life of usefulness, and shut himself off from the constant overflow of joy and peace that comes through obedience and submission. At the most inopportune moment, the sheep will bleat and the oxen will bellow—so stay close to the Lord.

Jerry: He took upon himself the duty of a priest–he was no priest. He had no right to offer sacrifice. Yet, he took God's work in his own hands.

Steve: Disobedience to God was another serious blunder he made. It is always serious when anyone turns away from God. His jealousy toward young David was tragic.

Danny: Jealousy was deep-seated in the king. He must have been afraid David would one day take his throne. He just didn't want this to happen. *Fear* of David bugged him no end.

Jerry: Saul was a selfish, ambitious man, and he was not willing to divide allegiance with any other. Saul was a wicked man. Murder was not out of line for him–in addition to a desire to kill David, Saul had 85 priests killed. Saul was on the stupid side for not staying close to Samuel, the prophet of the Lord. He was there to help the king go straight. It would have but he missed it.

Steve: In some respects Saul was both a success and a failure. The message from Samuel that Saul and his sons would die the next day shook Saul up. Saul's biggest blunder was when he turned his back on God.

Ann: One sin doesn't cover up another. Saul attempted this but to no avail.

Jake: Saul had everything going for him at first. He was anointed by God, the people were behind him, the prophet could keep him directed for the day. He wanted to stay down as the people's king but he blew it.

Danny: Fear, jealousy, ambition, and selfishness conquered a guy who had everything going for him. Saul had every advantage to make a great king.

Harry: Samuel was as close to Saul as he was allowed to be. Saul was so preoccupied with his selfish concerns during his entire reign that he had no time for spiritual things: he never consulted God about anything.

Wallie: "Saul" is alive today. He goes to the mountains, lakes, resorts, golf courses every weekend. He is too busy with business and pleasure to have time for God and worship.

Mike: Some mow the lawns, do the wash, "sack in" all day Sunday.

Gennie: Saul failed to consider his family, his friends, or his people in the wrong decisions he made; not one time did he consider his responsibility to them in his wrong choice. His mistakes not only affected him but others as well.

Lucy: Saul didn't plan to be the failure that he was. He had no idea that his life and that of his sons would come to such a tragic end. But he didn't plan it differently, so he had a tragic end. A person has to decide some things. He has to plan for them or it may not happen.

Jerry: A serious-minded person had better decide before making a decision whether it would glorify God or self. If it is God's will, it will glorify him. I need to ask *why* I am doing what I am.

Ada: Saul is one character I wouldn't want to be like, so I must continually seek the will of God for my life in everything I do.

Steve: Each morning we must die to self and let the Lord live his life through us daily.

Jerry: I find it helpful to begin every day with my Bible and then make a fresh commitment of my life to God as I begin the day, seeking his guidance for the day. Most of Saul's decisions he made without seeking the Lord's will. Not until after it was too late did he seek the Lord.

LESSONS FROM SAUL

Saul was so human that he speaks to every one of us. We identify in so many ways, especially in weaknesses and mistakes. Saul had access to the will of God every hour of the day through the good prophet Samuel. He had no excuse for most of his tragic mistakes.

Although God didn't want his people to have a king, Saul was God's choice since the people demanded one. Being God's choice and an excellent soldier, with the help of Samuel, Saul had every reason in the world to succeed as king. But Saul was presumptuous, jealous, and selfish. He disregarded the Word of God, took priestly responsibilities into his own hands, and God had to cut him down.

Saul was a disappointment to both Samuel and God. We should learn a lesson from Saul as to what jealousy, ambition, and pride will lead to. David's victories that should have been pleasing to the king proved to put Saul's character to the test.

And too, we see from Saul what wrong attitudes can lead to. Saul's son had to take a stand against his father, in favor of his young friend, David.

From Saul we learn that being brought up with a silver spoon in your mouth doesn't guarantee happiness or success. Even though Saul came to be one of the richest men in the world, he was never really a happy man. He had anything that money could buy, but happiness cannot be bought. Saul died a failure.

We should remember, also, that Saul started out in life with a religious background. He loved people. He knew the Jewish faith. He knew the Ten Commandments, but evil temptation lured him away from God.

During the early part of his reign, Saul tried to destroy all the mediums because he knew they were against God's will. But we learn that before he died he had turned to one.

Saul speaks to us today. If we will only profit by his mistakes. "So Saul died for his transgression, which he committed against the Lord, even against the word of the Lord, which he kept not, and also for asking counsel of one that had a familiar spirit, to inquire of it; and inquired not of the Lord: therefore he slew him, and turned the kingdom unto David the son of Jesse" (1 Chron. 10:13-14.)

God finally turned against Saul, after Saul had turned on him. The devil mastered Saul as he did Judas. Saul turned to witches. To the amazement of Saul and the witch of Endor God *allowed* him a message from the Lord. After losing all connection with God, he turned to other media.

Saul had failed God so he suffered the consequences. To save the shame and disgrace, Saul took his own life with his own sword.

Saul is the example of one who could have, but didn't. In addition to his other wicked acts, he had 85 priests of the Lord killed in an effort to stamp out religion. He failed when he could have succeeded.

"The saddest words of tongue or pen are these—it might have been."

SPIRITUAL THERAPY

To get the most personal benefit from this character study, take a pencil and a sheet of paper and answer the following questions.

1. What were the strong points or characteristics of the character? List them on paper.

2. What were the weaknesses of this character? List them.

3. What did the character have going for him or her? List the things in his favor.

4. What decisions or choices did the character make that you think were wrong? List the wrong ones, then list the right ones.

5. How can you benefit by your study of this character?

6. Have you really been face to face with yourself?

Notes:

5
Remember Her
(Lot's Wife)
Genesis 19

There are two women mentioned in the Bible that our Lord said, "Remember!" One is in the Old Testament—the other is in the New. One is to be commended—the other is to be pitied. One was a good woman—the other was worldly.

The good woman of the New Testament we are asked to remember took an alabaster box and anointed Jesus from his head to his feet with the precious ointment, a pound of pure nard. She wiped his feet with the hair of her head. Jesus said, "Wheresoever the gospel is preached in the whole world, this act, done by this woman, should be told as a memorial to her." "Remember her," said Jesus.

The Old Testament character Jesus wanted us to "remember" was the wife of Lot, the mayor of Sodom. In Luke 17:32 Jesus said, "Remember Lot's wife." Her Bible record is found in the book of Genesis. You might do well to read Genesis 19 before reading this chapter.

You will recall Abraham was called of God to come up out of Ur of the Chaldees. Lot, a nephew of Abraham, evidently came along with him. After getting into the land, God prospered both of them with an increase in cattle and goods. Their herdsmen were continually complaining about the better grass, the better pastures, and who would get this or that well.

Abraham was a gracious and generous man with a great heart. One day he said to his nephew, "Lot, we can't have this complaining and arguing among our herdsmen. You take your choice, I'll give you the benefit of the doubt; you decide which way you will go, and I'll take what's left." And yet God had not promised Lot a thing–God had promised Abraham all the land. Generous soul that he was, Abraham wanted no trouble.

Lot, a selfish man, looked toward the fertile plains of the Jordan–toward Sodom. And so Lot decided, "I'll take the fertile plains down toward the valley." Abraham accepted what was left, and each went his way.

Now, "Lot pitched his tent toward Sodom," the Bible says. Surely he didn't intend to end up in Sodom, but he did. Life is like that. People do not intend to do those evil sins that come to pass. Lot didn't intend to go to Sodom, but he started in that direction. After starting in that direction, it was difficult for him to stop.

In the second book of Peter the Bible says, "Lot sat in the gates of that wicked city and vexed his righteous soul day by day." God saw the wickedness of the city. The stench of sin came up to his nostrils and he said, "I'm going to destroy Sodom."

Lot and his family were in the wicked city and God said, "I won't destroy Sodom without first telling Abraham." The reason God wanted to tell Abraham was that "Abraham commands his children." Well, you would think that God wanted to tell Abraham because his nephew, Lot, was in Sodom. Right, I think that had something to do with it, but God said in his Word that he would tell Abraham, because he was a man who commanded his children.

When God warned Abraham that he would destroy Sodom, Abraham replied, "Lord, you would not destroy the good people that live in Sodom, would you?" There is a question as to whether there were any good people in Sodom. But there was Lot who had come with him from Ur of the Chaldees.

Lot, who had lived with his uncle, had seen the altars built to God, he had heard the message from God, and he had taken part in the offerings and matters pertaining to the worship and service of God, Jehovah. Yet he was in Sodom vexing his soul, his righteous soul, from day to day.

Abraham pled, "Lord you won't destroy the righteous, will

you, with the city?" Then Abraham said, "If I can find fifty righteous, would you save the city?" And you know how this dialogue went. God said, "If I can find fifty." God didn't leave it to Abraham to find fifty–God said, "If I can find fifty."

Then Abraham pleaded with God again and again. He pleaded with God until he got down to ten. But ten righteous persons couldn't be found in all Sodom! Where was righteous Lot? Where was his family? Where were the people that supposedly were children of God in Sodom? Their influence, where was it? What had they done? How had they lived? Only three people escaped the city and into the mountains alive–only three.

God sent two men, angels, into the city to prepare Lot and his family for the destruction of Sodom. They would have a chance to get out. The two men seemed to plan to stay on the street overnight, but Lot insisted that they tarry in his house. They finally agreed to go to his home.

The people in the city saw these strangers–they didn't know they were two angels from God–go into Lot's house, and they didn't like it. So, during the night they formed a mob, went to Lot's house, and demanded that the two men be brought out. Lot made every kind of proposition that he could make. He even offered his two innocent daughters to the mob, the angry men outside, if they would simply go away and leave the strangers alone. Finally the mob would have overcome Lot, but the angels reached for him and pulled him back through the door. The angels smote blind all the men in the mob outside and shut the door. They then asked Lot, "Do you have any here besides?" They knew that Lot had sons in the city, and daughters in the city, sons-in-law, and also two unwed girls there in the home. And the angels said, "Do you have any here besides sons, sons-in-law, your wife, and these two girls?"

The picture is sad–the Bible reveals Lot going to the homes of his daughters in the wee hours of the morning, when he should have been asleep. But he couldn't sleep. God was going to destroy the city the next morning at the rising of the sun, and Lot knew it. The sons-in-law, the Bible leads us to believe, sneered at the man. They chided him. They ridiculed him. They called him a joke. They let him know that they had no confidence whatsoever in his life, or in his word, or in his testimony. He seemed as "one to mock" to those who knew him best.

The Bible recorded Lot's attitude in these words: "He lingered." But is it any wonder he lingered? His children would burn with the wicked city. Who would have wanted to go off and leave loved ones to burn in a few hours? The Scripture says, "While he lingered, the angels laid hands upon him." They literally dragged him out of the city, saying, "Don't look back. For God is going to rain hail, fire, and brimstone upon this city." And the Bible depicts the whole story.

Evidently Mrs. Lot was lagging behind. The Scripture says, "But Lot's wife looked back from behind him, and she became a pillar of salt." But she had been warned, plenty. Lot and his two daughters went on into the mountains. Read the rest of this tragic story in chapter nineteen of Genesis. What happened between Lot and his two daughters is too sad to write! These girls made their daddy drunk, and became pregnant by him.

LESSONS TO REMEMBER

People set their own sails. The time comes when everyone must take sides. This choice is a must. God puts both life and death before everyone and each must decide whether it will be life or death. Mrs. Lot made her choice, but it was a tragic one. No one should follow her example. People decide their own fate, and no one can be blamed for it. Jesus said, "Remember Lot's wife." Let's never forget that the wrath of God awaits those who spurn, reject, and defy his will.

There is danger and tragedy of divided loyalty. Divided loyalty is one of the major tragedies in the modern church. People try to hold onto God with one hand, and to the world with the other. This is impossible, though some try it. All too many times it is too late when they realize their doom. "Remember Lot's wife!" Look around you for people who are making this mistake. Dare not do it yourself.

In the eyes of the Sodomites, Mrs. Lot was "somebody." She was involved in all the social life of her city. It would do us good to remember some of the events and influences for good that could have been a blessing to her, yet she failed to heed them.

This woman had been under the influence of the great and noble Abraham. She had seen his example of dedication, devotion, and worship of Jehovah. Lot himself "vexed his righteous soul from day to day." That should have been a good influence on her, yet it failed.

The angels came to inform and warn her of the horror that awaited those who remained in the city, but Lot's wife did not heed this advice. These angels dragged her out of the city and warned her. "Don't look back" but she disobeyed. The only thing left was the sad circumstance, "A pillar of salt."

We should remember that Satan doesn't fulfill his promises. He is cunning, shrewd, but watch him. He is a liar from the beginning. Don't let him pull the wool over your eyes. When the laws of God are spurned, you may expect moral decay, and God destroyed Sodom for such wickedness. God has not changed; his attitude toward sin has not changed. Sin must be adequately dealt with.

Let us learn from this mayor's wife that, "Where your treasure is, your heart will be also." This fact is evident daily in the lives of people. Jesus knew that this was true—therefore, he urged that we be sure that our chief treasure is laid up in heaven.

From this story we learn that there is dire danger in *profession* without *possession.* The new birth is absolutely essential to a life dedicated to the will of God. "That which is born of the flesh is flesh"—and nothing else can come from it. Only the spiritual birth can put a person into the will of God.

Men must never forget that God's Spirit will not strive always with man. Ample time was given Lot and his family to leave the city. There comes a time when the Almighty will turn loose wicked people, take off the bridle of restraint, and leave them to destroy themselves. Don't risk it. Lot's wife did. Jesus cautioned, "Remember her."

God grows tired with people who continue to profess and never give evidence of the genuine possession. Hypocrisy is an abomination to God. "Let a man examine himself."

Some people dedicate themselves to an inferior list of priorities, not realizing the awful outcome in the end. We can't give in. We can't compromise. Let's examine our priorities before it's too late. This could be the reason for such a difference in the dedication of some.

The value of a good Christian home should come to our attention, as we study Lot's home. Whether or not Mrs. Lot "vexed her righteous soul from day to day," as the Bible says her husband did, we do not know. We do know that confidence and trust were not listed among the assets of that home. Children didn't trust parents, wife didn't trust husband, and all went wrong.

Lot and his wife missed God's design for a godly home. Unlike Abraham who "commanded his children," Lot's children had no confidence in him. Abraham's life before his children led them to respect and confidence. As Edgar Guest observed, "It takes a heap of living in a house to make a home."

The Bible command, "Honor thy father and thy mother," indicates that parents should be honorable. Then, children are to honor them. Honor must be earned. It comes with a price tag.

It is not likely that Lot intended to end up in the wicked city of Sodom. People never do. That father who took his first social drink had no thought of finally becoming a slave to strong drink, debauching his life, losing his family, and ending up on the rocks. That mother who decided only to pitch her tent toward Sodom didn't intend to end up on the altar of sin. That beautiful young girl who decided to share her body once to see what the "kick" is all about, had no thought of ending up in the "red-light district."

My word of caution is, if you don't intend to end up in Sodom, then don't pitch your tent in that direction.

Let me conclude this study of Lot's wife by reminding you of the final curse–the doom–of a divided heart. It makes for Christian anemia; it cripples one's work for Christ. It retards progress. It forfeits one's Christian influence, and in the end, it is destruction. For Lot's wife, it was a statue of salt to forever remind others of its tragedy. Good intentions are fine, but, as the saying goes, "Hell is full of people with good intentions." God wants more. He wants genuine resolves, commitment, dedication, surrender–nothing less!

SPIRITUAL THERAPY

To get the most personal benefit from this character study, take a pencil and a sheet of paper and answer the following questions.

1. What were the strong points or characteristics of the character? List them on paper.

2. What were the weaknesses of this character? List them.

3. What did the character have going for him or her? List the things in his favor.

4. What decisions or choices did the character make that you think were wrong? List the wrong ones, then list the right ones.

5. How can you benefit by your study of this character?

6. Have you really been face to face with yourself?

Notes:

6
Costly Disloyalties
(Jacob)
Genesis 28:1-49:33

Let me introduce you to a young man who was too crooked to stay in the tent of his father. His crime was so great that he became a fugitive from justice. For a long time, this trickster was not even a halfway honest man. His name indicates that he was a trickster, a surplanter, a shrewd "con man," even one who stooped low enough to cheat his own brother out of the family birthright.

By now you have discovered his name—Jacob. Even though his brother, Esau, was rather animalistic and seemed to have no regard for the finer things of life, Jacob's treatment of him reveals that Jacob himself was in no sense an "upstanding gentleman."

When Jacob left his home in Canaan to escape the wrath of Esau, his angry brother, Rebekah, their mother, expected that soon Esau's anger would cease, and her favorite son, Jacob, could return home. But such was not the case. Jacob never again saw his mother, who had connived to help him receive his father's blessing—a blessing that ordinarily went to the eldest son.

En route to his Uncle Laban's in Haran, Jacob the young vagabond had an amazing experience. Before sunset one evening, as he ambled along trying to decide where to stop for the night, Jacob discovered a lovely place among the mountains, barely beyond the border of the desert. Since he had no bed on which to lie, he took a stone, rested his head on it for a pillow, and prepared himself for a night's rest. Having walked long and hard all day, he was tired and soon fell asleep.

That night, while Jacob rested his head on a rock pillow, God came to him in a vision. He saw a ladder that stretched from heaven down to the earth. The lower end of the ladder reached all the way to where he was sleeping. Going up and down, from earth to heaven and back to earth, were angels. And at the top of the ladder a gate opened to heaven. Standing in the open door was the Lord God.

He spoke to Jacob. It was music in Jacob's ears to hear the Lord say, "Jacob, I am the Lord, the God of Abraham, and the God of Isaac, your father: I will be your God, too. The land where you are lying is yours, and it will belong to your children after you: If you look east, west, north, and south, you will see what is yours." Then he promised, "Jacob, through you and your family I am going to bless the world." He further covenanted, "Jacob, I will go with you, I will be with you, and I will never leave you, and you can depend on my promise."

As the first rays of the early morning sun broke through the night, Jacob awoke from his sleep. Something had happened; Jacob had never been so happy. Thinking that he was all alone and away from home, Jacob had discovered that God was with him in that place. *God was with him!* Before he could leave on his journey to his uncle's, he named the place where God revealed himself, "Bethel," for to Jacob, it was indeed "the house of God."

After naming the place "Bethel," Jacob made a vow to God. He made this promise: "If God will be with me, and will keep me in this way that I go, and will give me bread to eat, and will bring me to my father's house in peace, then the Lord shall be my God; and this stone shall be the house of God; and of all that God gives me, I will give back to him one tenth."

After this remarkable experience with the God of his fathers, Jacob enjoyed his journey to Laban's house. At the end of his trip Jacob had at last reached the famous well by the city. He had heard his mother, Rebekah, speak about the well so many times. For, it was at that same well that the chief servant of Abraham, his grandfather, first met Rebekah, and brought her back to Canaan, where she became the wife of Isaac.

As he approached the well, the runaway lad saw in the distance a young woman coming, bringing her sheep to water. Something within the young man, perhaps his upbringing, urged him to water the sheep for her. So, Jacob lifted off from the curb the flat stone that covered the mouth of the well, drew water, and gave it to the sheep. To his great surprise and joy, he found that the young woman, Rachel, was his first cousin. It was to her father's house that Jacob's mother had sent him.

It was love at first sight. Jacob immediately wanted Rachel for his wife. So, he lost no time. As soon as he had become acquainted with his mother's brother and his family, he bargained a deal with him. Jacob offered to work seven years for him if Laban would grant Rachel to him for a wife. To the offer Laban replied, "It is better that you have her than for a stranger to marry her." Jacob understood this to be a pact.

The seven years Jacob tended his uncle's flocks, his sheep and oxen, seemed but a few days to him, for Jacob was desperately in love with Rachel. At the end of the first seven years, Jacob, as a servant to his uncle, learned that Laban was not trustworthy. The time had come for him to have Rachel as his wife. The wedding was planned and Jacob was overcome with joy.

In those days the bride was covered with a veil until after the wedding. When Jacob lifted the veil to view the beautiful Rachel, whom he loved and had waited and worked for, he discovered that he had married Rachel's older sister, Leah. No greater blow had come to him since his brother, Esau, had threatened his life.

A trickster had been tricked. As he had cheated on his father and his brother, at last the chickens had come home to roost. Jacob was furious and made his anger known to his uncle, only to have Laban explain, "In our country the youngest daughter never marries until after the older ones have married."

Not willing to be outdone, Jacob offered to work until he got the girl he loved. After working for his uncle seven additional years, Jacob married Rachel. Although Jacob had eleven sons born to him in Haran, Rachel had only one child for Jacob, and they named him Joseph. This son was the one Jacob loved the most. For one reason, he was the youngest—but more than that, he was Jacob's son by Rachel whom he also loved dearly.

When he arrived at Haran, Jacob had no idea of staying there so many years. It was his intention, and that of his mother, for him to return home as soon as Esau had time to forget the wrong Jacob had done to him. They wanted to give Esau time to cool off and forget.

As pay for his labor, Jacob took sheep, oxen, and camels from Laban. In this manner, Jacob grew richer and richer, year by year, for the Lord seemed to bless everything his hands touched. At the end of twenty years in Haran, Jacob was considered a wealthy man. It was then that he decided to reunite with his father, Isaac, who was aged and most feeble. His mother, Rebekah, was no longer living.

For fear of what Laban would do, Jacob did not announce that he was leaving. One day when Laban was gone from home, Jacob gathered his family, his sheep, oxen, and camels—and fled. Of course, when his uncle returned to find them gone, he was outraged. Fearing that kind of response, Jacob was not at all surprised to see Laban coming to overtake him, and by force to make him go back to Haran.

Jacob was forever grateful to the Lord, because when Laban rode up to the camp near Mount Gilead, he kindly greeted the family. Laban later explained that the Lord had appeard to him the night before and asked him to deal considerately with Jacob and his family. You see, Jacob's two wives were Laban's daughters, and their children were his grandchildren.

Like two good men should, they made an agreement that day never to harm each other. Jacob's uncle kissed his daughters, then he kissed his grandchildren, and bid them "goodbye." He returned to Haran, and Jacob and his caravan headed for Canaan.

As they journeyed toward the old home place, Jacob got the scare of his life. Word reached him that his brother, Esau, with four hundred soldiers, was coming to meet him. Jacob could never forget how angry Esau became the day he returned from the hunt to find that Jacob connivingly had received the double portion blessing from his blind father, Isaac. He also knew that he could be no match for Esau and his soldiers, if Esau were still angry.

All of those years–twenty of them–Jacob had lived in fear of Esau. Jacob was sensitively aware of the wrong he had done Esau. Not only was Jacob's life at stake, he had his entire family with him. For fear that Esau would kill them, too, Jacob sent ahead to Esau a big portion of goods, hoping to buy him over. The gifts he sent him included oxen and cows, sheep and goats, camels and asses. All this Jacob did with the hope that he could appease the anger of his brother.

In addition to sending Esau those gifts, Jacob prayed all night before he was to meet him the next day. It was during this all-night prayer meeting that God really changed the trickster's life. God gave him a new name, also. Up until that night, the supplanter had lived up to his name, "Jacob," which means "trickster," "supplanter," But God changed Jacob's name to "Israel," which means "a prince who prevailed with God."

After crossing over the little brook, Kedron, the next morning, Israel looked up and saw Esau standing before him. They were face to face after all of those years. As was the custom for one to do before a superior, Jacob bowed before his older brother several times, after which Esau embraced him and placed kisses on his brow. The brothers wept together. As God had already done, Esau had forgiven Jacob of his wrong.

After much persuasion on the part of Jacob–now Israel–Esau took his family and settled in a portion of territory to the southeast called Edom. Jacob went with his family to Shechem in the land of Canaan.

Esau and Jacob met again when they buried their father, Isaac, in the cave at Hebron where their grandfather Abraham and their grandmother Sarah were buried years before.

Even though God had changed his life, and his name, Jacob's trouble had not ceased. While living in Shechem, Jacob's little daughter, Dinah, was seduced by the son of Hamor the Hivite.

And to make the matter even worse, two of his sons, Simon and Levi, killed all the men of the city, to get revenge for what had happened to their sister. It became so serious that Jacob was afraid for his own life and the lives of his family.

During these tragic times God communicated with Jacob. He ordered him to go back to Bethel, the place where he first had the vision of God standing in the gate of heaven. Having had enough of the old life, Jacob commanded all that were in his house to gather all the strange gods and prepare for a funeral. At his command the members of his family brought to him all the trinkets that had been used in idol worship. Jacob led his family out to a huge oak tree nearby. Under the tree they buried every idol that was in the camp. Then, they headed back to Bethel.

To Jacob, it was really "El Bethel," which means "the God of the house," for it was there that God appeared to him when he was running from Esau.

When Jacob left his Uncle Laban in Haran, he had only eleven boys, but at last Rachel had borne him a twelfth. She was the mother of his two favorite sons, Joseph and Benjamin. Of all his family, Jacob loved Rachel, Joseph, and Benjamin the best. For Rachel, he had worked fourteen years because of his intense love. But now Jacob had to face sorrow again, for soon after Benjamin came, Rachel died. The death of Rachel brought deep sorrow to his soul. Along the roadside, between Jerusalem and Bethlehem, he laid the body of his precious Rachel to rest. At the time Joseph was seventeen, and Benjamin was the baby of the family.

Life to Jacob was one trouble after another. Not long after his wife died, Joseph, his most precious son, was sold into slavery by his brothers. There were not many days during his life, after he was party to the deception planned by his mother, that his sin did not find him out. Had Jacob known the outcome from the beginning, his life would have been lived differently. It was more than he could bear to think of never again seeing his dearest son, Joseph. Jacob lived to attest to the fact: "Be not deceived,

God is not mocked and whatsoever a man soweth, that shall he also reap."

But in due time in a miraculous way, God united his family by promoting Joseph to the second in command of Egypt. The Lord spoke to him and said: "Jacob, I am the Lord, the God of your father, fear not to go down to Egypt; for I will go down with you; and there you shall see your son Joseph; and in Egypt I will make of your descendants a great people. And I will surely bring them back again to this land." At last, Jacob had found his most beloved son, and they were to be reunited.

With sixty-six children and grandchildren, Jacob loaded up the caravan and headed for Egypt to see his long-lost son.

Upon their arrival in Egypt, Joseph rode in the king's chariot to meet his father. When they met, Joseph fell upon Jacob's neck and wept. It was then that Jacob really came to know how Rebekah felt when her favorite son left home, not to return until after her death.

Even though Jacob and his family had been reunited with Joseph, they were in a strange land. God had promised Jacob the land of Canaan, and there he wanted to die. Not knowing how long his sojourn would last in Egypt, Jacob instructed his sons to take his body with them when they left Egypt.

Among the last acts of importance that Jacob did was to pass his blessing on to the two sons of Joseph. When Joseph brought his two sons, Manasseh and Ephraim, to his bedside, Jacob's eyes were dim with age, as were Isaac's when he gave him the blessing. Jacob couldn't see his two grandsons, but when Joseph told him that they were his, the old man reached his hands out to them. Remembering how his blind father, Isaac, had placed his feeble hands upon his head, Jacob did the same to the two sons of Joseph. With his right hand upon the head of Ephraim, the younger, and his left hand on Manasseh, Jacob was ready to give the blessing to them. Thinking that his father was mistaken, Joseph made an attempt to change the hands of Jacob, so that his right hand would be on the older son's head. Not allowing him to do so, Jacob explained that he knew what he was doing. Jacob realized that in the future Ephraim would become greater and more powerful than Manasseh. Feeling that his work on earth had come to an end, Jacob patiently waited for the Lord to come for him.

FACE TO FACE . . . WITH YOURSELF

Most of us that read this fascinating story about Jacob, who later became Israel, can see ourselves as we read. Jacob was like so many of us–human. He had high ambitions, but with the help of a scheming mother, it was easy for him to follow the baser motives that seemed to at times overwhelm him.

More so than in most characters, Jacob is an example of the outcome of misplaced trust and of extravagant disloyalties.

In this man is to be found an example of what God can do with, in, and through the worst of us, if he is only given a chance to do so. God took Jacob, a conniver, and made him into a prince. This God did only when Jacob was willing to be made over. Jacob had to reach his extremity before God could become his opportunity.

Jacob, like so many people, played around with his duty to God until he was faced with a serious and dangerous experience. For twenty years he had played loose with his responsibility to God, all the time wondering how he could ever right the wrong that he had done to his older brother, Esau. Jacob could never forget his experience with God at Bethel that first night away from home. Twenty years had passed, his mother had died, his father was senile and feeble–yet, he was still afraid to face Esau.

Following his total commitment to the Lord in an all-night prayer meeting, Jacob not only got a name change, he received a new heart as well. Having been changed from a cheat to a prince who had power with God, Jacob no longer feared what would happen to him. Such a transformation will make a conqueror out of any coward.

How can the study of Jacob's life make your life more fruitful? What are some things that would have been different if Jacob had let God lead him in all of his decisions?

SELF-ANALYSIS

Richard: One of the things that has impressed me most in the study of Jacob is the fact that the wrong choice or decision not only brings hurt to the one who makes it–others suffer also. For this reason, I have resolved to be more careful and prayerful about the choices I make in the future.

Larry: That's right. It is certainly true that no man lives to himself and no man dies to himself. I have always heard it said that one person will profit from the other fellow's mistakes, but if I keep my right mind, I'm surely going to profit by some that Jacob made.

Patty: Jacob should have learned from his mother, Rachel, that it doesn't pay to cheat, but she taught him to do so.

Bob: It is amazing what God can do for and with a life, no matter how wicked and selfish it may have been, that yields to him. It was difficult for Jacob, and he was a long time coming to it.

When he crossed the little brook, Jabbok, that night, his mind was made up–whatever the cost, no matter what, Jacob had come to himself, and he was ready to follow the Lord. It was that night after wrestling all night with God that Jacob gave up to Him. He had "had it." Enough was enough. At last God had won. When Jacob confessed his sins, God forgave him. He did more– he changed Jacob's name to Israel. Self had been conquered, God had been enthroned in his life.

Frank: Just think, this is what happens to every person who, like Jacob, surrenders himself to God's will. This can happen to anyone who has never had this transforming experience.

Jim: It's great to see the life of Jacob so changed by the power of God, but it would have been so much better if it could have happened years before, even before Jacob sowed so many wild oats that had to spring up and reap their harvest. Although Jacob had made peace with the Lord, he had to face all the bad results of the seed he had sown. It broke his heart day by day. If he could say one thing to us, young and old, it would be: Don't waste your life. Give it to God early.

CONCLUSIONS

The person always trying to bargain with God never gets as much as he would if he simply trusted him. It really doesn't pay to make bargains with the Lord.

So much of Jacob, most of us see in ourselves. He is a twin brother to some of us. You find him in every crowd. He sits in the pew at church. He sings in the choir. He stands behind the pulpit. He eats at the average table.

To stand before the full mirror of Jacob's life you can take a good look at yourself. How much of yourself do you see in Jacob?

It is sad to discover that the house in which Jacob grew up had a serious division. This had its bad effect on him as a youth. The father favored the older Esau, while the mother favored the younger Jacob. This in itself was a bad influence on Jacob.

Sooner or later every person will reap the harvest of his sins.

As Jacob had deceived his father, his own sons deceived him.

Jacob is an example of one who never would let God choose for him.

Remember! Your attitude toward God's ways will make or break you. "The ways of the Lord are straight."

Jacob's first vow to God was made on the condition that, "If God will be with me, and keep and clothe me, then shall the Lord be my God." The rest of his life he spent driving bargains. He lost every time.

As you see yourself through the life of Jacob, remember that God cannot allow our deception to go unnoticed. Punishment must follow.

God never breaks his promise to us: we often break ours.

A man out of fellowship with God is always a coward. Jacob is proof.

In the end Jacob confessed, "Few and evil have been my days." He died in exile.

The Bible says: "He that covereth his sin shall not prosper." For twenty years Jacob lived away from the will of God–he finally took his stand, led his family to bury their idols under a tree, and headed for Bethel.

If you are living in a "strange land" so far as the will of God is concerned, why not profit by Jacob's mistakes and waste no more time. Put your life on the line for God. Some wait too late to do this, and loved ones are influenced to procrastinate.

All too many wander off into a far country of sin; if they return, they still leave some of their family in that condition.

Like Jacob, a life of planning and scheming brings nothing but exile and dread.

Happy is the person–when finally forced to ford the Jabbok–if he crosses over with a broken and contrite heart, willing to be broken in submission to the will of God.

Don't put this character out of your mind until you are reminded once again of Jacob's looking upon the blood-smeared "coat of many colors" that belonged to his favorite son, Joseph. Hear his mournful words: "I will go down to the grave unto my son mourning." Remember, too, that the coat he held in his hands was a reminder to Jacob of the workings of the law of God's judgment and retribution. Payday had come.

Happy is the person who can profit by Jacob's mistakes, so he will never find it necessary to repeat these words, "As I have done, so the Lord hath requited me."

No matter what the past had been with Joseph, no matter what your past has been, like him you can begin life over by complete submission to God's will. You, too, can become a prince or princess, who can have power with God and men."

1. Disloyalties come at a tremendous cost.

2. Be sure your sins will find you out.

3. The sins of the father visit and haunt the second and third generations. "Like father, like son."

4. You might be forgiven for the sin, but you can't stop the outcome.

5. Some who go off into a "far country" of sin return, but too many times they take loved ones with them who don't get back.

6. Seeming success in one sin venture leads to another and another.

7. Funeral for disloyalties may hurt, but it's the only safe way out.

8. When Jacob got right with God and proved the same to his family, they followed him back to Bethel.

9. It is difficult for children to find Bethel when parents are so far from it.

10. Funerals may be necessary on the road from Shechem to Bethel, but they are worth it, and sometimes necessary.

SPIRITUAL THERAPY

To get the most personal benefit from this character study, take a pencil and a sheet of paper and answer the following questions.

1. What were the strong points or characteristics of the character? List them on paper.

2. What were the weaknesses of this character? List them.

3. What did the character have going for him or her? List the things in his favor.

4. What decisions or choices did the character make that you think were wrong? List the wrong ones, then list the right ones.

5. How can you benefit by your study of this character?

6. Have you really been face to face with yourself?

Notes:

7
A Great Woman
(The Shunammite Woman)
2 Kings 4

God had to be the author of the Bible—only God would reveal the bad, as well as the good, and the good as well as the bad, about the people of the Bible.

The Bible contains good facts about good people and sometimes it records evil about the same people. There are only a few characters mentioned in Holy Writ whose flaws are not mentioned. This does not mean that they had no wrong in their lives, for the Bible teaches otherwise. "There is none righteous, no, not one" (Rom. 3:10). "For all have sinned, and come short of the glory of God" (Rom. 3:23).

Very little space in the Bible is taken up with the character in this chapter. However, what is written is extremely important.

So far as I can find, this is the only woman in the Bible who is labeled by Jehovah as "a great woman." For this and other reasons, I have chosen to write about the Shunammite woman. She has been an inspiration to many. The Bible is neither extravagant nor wasteful with words. When God called this woman "great," he meant just that.

Since I was nine years old, this woman of Shunem has to me afforded one of the most fascinating stories in the Bible. My Sunday School quarterly, when I was a kid, had a picture of the prophet's chamber which was on top of the house where the woman of Shunem and her husband lived.

One Sunday decades ago, I learned the story of her life. The room upon the flat roof of her home was not an oddity to me when I learned what it was and why it was built there.

You see, in our community there were two of our church families who had what they called "the prophet's chamber" in their homes. Our preacher went to college all week, and on Saturday he would ride the train to the closest town, where one of these two families met the train for him. The preacher had his own private room in each of these homes where he was entertained over the weekend.

During the day of Elisha, a farm couple lived in the community of Shunem. Little do we know about the couple, for their names are not recorded in the Bible. The man is identified with the reapers of the field; the woman is called the Shunammite by the servant of God, Elisha.

The Bible introduces our character on this wise: "And it fell on a day, that Elisha passed to Shunem, where was a great woman; and she constrained him to eat bread. And so it was, as often as he passed by, he turned in thither to eat bread" (2 Kings 4:8).

Without identification, the Bible continues the story. This woman classified as "great" discussed the matter with her husband, at the time the only other member of the family. Out of sympathy and concern for the man of God and Gehazi, his servant, the good lady discussed with her husband what they could do to make matters better for the prophet.

Traveling, most of the time on foot, from one part of the country to the other, the prophet and his servant passed that way often. This woman the Bible calls "great" had a vision of what they could do, more than refresh the preacher with food and drink. The woman's husband may have been one of the better farmers of his generation, but the home in which the couple lived must have been too small for frequent company. So the woman made this suggestion: "Behold now, I perceive that this is an holy man of God, which passeth us continually. Let us make a little chamber, I pray thee, on the wall; and let us set for him there a bed, and a table, and a stool, and a candlestick: and it shall be, when he cometh to us, that he shall turn in thither" (2 Kings 4:9-10).

The Bible does not record further conversation between the

husband and wife concerning her suggestion. It does, however, picture Elisha and Gehazi as using the prophet's chamber from time to time. It is likely that without loss of time, the woman's husband prepared the "room on the wall."

One day, as the two weary men of God relaxed in the little room, the prophet decided that one good turn prompts another. Out of gratitude to the kind Shunammite couple, he would return the favor.

With this in mind, Elisha commanded his servant to inquire of the lady if he could speak to the king on her behalf. Prophets like Elisha had prodigious weight with most of the kings of the day. A word from him could cinch the woman's husband a position in the king's court. At any rate, Elisha was willing to return her gracious favor.

When approached with the idea of his speaking to the king for her, the Shunammite woman replied without hesitation, "I dwell among my own people," as much as to say, "My home is my throne." At least he tried, but the prophet failed. The great woman was not interested in his suggestion.

The couple had no children, and evidently the woman—though her age is not mentioned in the Bible—was much younger than her husband, for the Bible does say, "The woman has no child, and her husband is old."

Baffled about what they could do to return her favor, Gehazi came up with the idea of a child for the couple. Her concern and care for them had given him the idea. In answer to the prophet's question, "What then is to be done for her?" Gehazi suggested that they ask God to grant her a child. Nothing could have pleased the great woman more. A baby boy was born to them in due season.

The Bible also indicates: "And when the child was grown [evidently about the age of twelve], it fell on a day, that he went out to his father to the reapers."

While the lad was in the field, he took seriously ill. He cried to his father, "My head, my head." Immediately the father sent the boy home to his mother. Sicker no doubt than his father had imagined, the boy "sat on her knee till noon, and then died." This is one of the most touching verses in the Bible.

This godly woman had not forgotten the little room on the roof, and its purpose. So, with the lifeless body of her child, she climbed the stairway to the roof, where she placed the boy's body on the prophet's bed.

Without wasting time, and without despair, her faith sent her in search of the prophet Elisha. When she reached sight of the man of God, he sent his servant to meet her to inquire about her business.

In keeping with the prophet's request, Gehazi met the woman with the question: "Is it well with thee?" Her reply was, "It is well." The prophet's second question was: "Is it well with thy husband?" The reply was the same. Then Elisha asked, "Is it well with the child?" At that moment the dead child, cold and stiff, was lying on the prophet's bed. Yet, the great woman answered, "It is well." Touched by the sadness of the mother, yet strengthened by her unshaken faith, the prophet went with her to Shunem.

Being lighter footed and speedier than the prophet, Gehazi went ahead with instructions from Elisha about what to do. Gehazi could do nothing about the child's condition.

When Elisha reached the prophet's chamber where lay the body of the dead child, he emptied the room of all but the body of the lad and himself. The Bible declares that he prayed to Jehovah. Then, he stretched himself out over the child, mouth to mouth, eyes to eyes, hands to hands. Getting up, he walked the floor in prayerful concern. Then going back, he stretched himself once again over the lifeless body. The child sneezed seven times, and then opened his eyes.

First calling in his servant, Elisha had Gehazi then summon the lad's mother. Arriving in the room, she saw her son alive; she fell at Elisha's feet, bowed herself to the floor, picked up her child, and went out.

This sad, but finally joyous, story is loaded with spiritual "appetizers." It has lessons galore.

The Shunammite woman was a *great woman* because she had a *great purpose* in life. A person without a purpose in life drifts aimlessly. If there is no real purpose in life, one is like a ship at sea in "The Bermuda Triangle." But a life with a purpose, with that purpose anchored in God, and with a desire to perform the will of God, cannot be destroyed. Though it may temporarily be shipwrecked, "It is well."

Evidently the woman's purpose was to have a great home. As goes the home, so goes the community. As goes the home, so goes the state, the nation, and the world. The very first institution that God fashioned for the benefit of the human race was the home. And here was a woman who latched onto that fact early in her life. She realized that to have a happy home, she would have to make a happy marriage. And that meant one man and one woman united together, becoming one in God by God's own power and authority. And so she married.

She and her husband didn't have children early, but they ministered to people. One of the chief delights of this couple was to minister to other people. They cared for others, they thought about others, they were interested in others. And it's manifested in the fact that they built the room for the prophet, which no doubt made room for other guests in another area of the house.

The Word of God is quiet at this point, so I will not speak where it does not speak. But this woman had a noble purpose to cultivate a good home. To do that, she had to live some in that house. "It takes a heap of living to make a house a home," said Edgar Guest. And so she did. When the prophet said that he would speak to the king for her, she replied, "Never mind, I have my work cut out for me." She had a mother's heart, even though she didn't have a child.

Another factor that made the woman "great" was her faith in God. God gave her a child, and when the boy had grown to be a dozen years old, he went to the field with his father. Nothing can mean more to a home than the kisses of a baby's lips and his "goo goo's" and "da da's" and "ma ma's." And later to hear that child call out, "Hi, Mom. Hey, Dad."

But their child died!

The woman did all she could. She wrestled with death until noon, and her boy died on her lap.

There is nothing wrong with babysitters. What I am going to mention is unfortunately not an isolated case. I know of one mother who left her sick baby and went to a party, and the child died while she was gone. Not so with this great Shunammite woman. She was there when she was needed, and she fought death as long as breath would give her strength. But the boy died.

She sought God's help through the prophet. When asked, "Is it well with thee?" she replied, "It is well." She answered, "It is well" to all of his questions. When he asked about the child, she still stated, "It is well," even though the child lay dead. Maybe she realized that God would raise up the child and give him back to her. Perhaps her faith was that firm. I do know that she felt her boy was in God's hands, and her faith was strong enough to understand that God's will would be accomplished. "Though he slay me, yet will I trust him" was Job's affirmation. The woman's faith was like that. And it's that kind of faith that leaves a matchless heritage to a child.

The Shunammite woman had a great faith and God presented her a great reward. Her child was raised from the dead after the woman put her faith into action. She trusted, but she also had done what she could. Most every man who achieves greatness gives considerable credit to his mother. Abraham Lincoln, whose mother died early in his life, said, "I owe all that I have and am to my mother."

Henry Grady, called the man who "loved our nation back to God in his generation," had just delivered a stirring message. Having swayed the audience, after pouring out his heart in love for his country and his fellowmen, the crowd sought him. When the people rushed down to applaud and praise him, they couldn't find him. He had slipped out through the back door. Down a long, winding road out into the country of Georgia, he went.

Finally, driving up to his mother's house, this stalwart man of nobility, character, prestige, renown, said, "Mom, your boy, your little boy, just got lonely to come home tonight. Mom, I want you to do just like you did when I was a little boy, I want you to take me to the bedroom, put me into the bed, tuck the cover about me, bend over your little boy tonight, and say your prayers for him, like you did when he was a child. Will you do that again tonight?"

Surely a mother would do that again, and she did. Could it be that you need to go back to your mother's knee? Maybe you need this challenge to your mother's knees again, where you can renew your faith in God, your mother's God.

Harriet Beecher Stowe wrote an undying tribute to the mother of the Beecher men. Of this great, noble family, she wrote: "Surely every one of her sons would, throughout their lives, give their mother's faith, their mother's holy life, and their mother's holy death credit for keeping them from the temptations of life."

It was the keeper of a penitentiary who said that a mother is the last person to give up on a child. He remarked, "I noticed through the years that friends, first of all, will forsake a person. Then, brothers or sisters will leave them. Then a wife—but last of all the mother would be holding out hope." Oh, the blessings of a Christian mother. I pay tribute to my wife—now in heaven—the mother of my children, and to my two daughters, now Christian mothers, too!

VALUABLE LESSONS FROM THIS GREAT WOMAN

Nancy: Good homes don't just happen. They come with a price tag. Someone in the home must pay that price. In this instance, it was the woman in the house. All too many are not willing to pay the price. We can learn a lesson from the Shunammite woman. I have decided that no price is too much for me to pay to have a good home.

Melody: I, too, have made a decision that will help me look for opportunities to be of service to those in need. God rewarded this woman and the joy she seemed to get from helping others was a reward in itself. God always outgives his children. I know my life will never be the same after seeing her example.

John: I'd like to remind us that, even though not much is said about the man of the house, we are led to believe that this good woman had his cooperation, or she could never have done what she did. Can't we give him some credit?

Pastor: You are right. For a home to be as happy as this one and to be as helpful, there must be oneness of purpose. This home had a unity. Homes like that are built upon trust, love, confidence, mutual understanding, and consideration. And even more important, God must have first place in the lives of those who make such homes.

Pam: I know some homes that God has not blessed with a child and yet those homes seem happy, because of their interest in and concern for others. They seem to live to make other people happy. From serving others, they must get great satisfaction.

Mary: Never before have I seen so much in the Bible. These characters we are studying are eye-openers to me. More and more, I am discovering myself–my real self. Could it be that I have never been willing to take a good look at myself, or is it that this is the first time I have been brought face to face with myself in so simple a way?

Judy: Mary isn't the only one in this group who feels this way. During these rap sessions with these Bible characters, I have come to a better understanding of and love for my parents and other members of my family. I can hardly wait to get home, I have so many things I want to talk over with them.

SPIRITUAL THERAPY

To get the most personal benefit from this character study, take a pencil and a sheet of paper and answer the following questions.

1. What were the strong points or characteristics of the character? List them on paper.

2. What were the weaknesses of this character? List them.

3. What did the character have going for him or her? List the things in his favor.

4. What decisions or choices did the character make that you think were wrong? List the wrong ones, then list the right ones.

5. How can you benefit by your study of this character?

6. Have you really been face to face with yourself?

Notes:

8
Judge, Prophet, and Priest
(Samuel)
1 Samuel 1:4-10:25

Every year countless Israelites made their pilgrimage to Shiloh. There they worshipped in "the house of the Lord" Joshua had moved from Gilgal. Samuel's parents were among those who made this worshipful journey, even for years before he was born. In fact, for years his mother, Hannah, was barren.

It was on one of those trips to the temple to worship and offer sacrifices that the Lord promised Hannah a child. She had stopped at the door of the Lord's temple to pray before entering to worship. For a long time, she had stood there, with her lips moving, but she was not uttering a sound. Eli, the high priest, approached her and reprimanded her, thinking that she was drunk or close to it.

When Eli found out that Hannah was not drunk, but that she was in distress because of her barrenness, he blessed her and let her go. The next day, Hannah, along with her husband, Elkanah, returned to the temple.

Before the child was born, Hannah named him Samuel, because she had asked God for him. Samuel literally means "heard of God."

While her baby was very young, Hannah didn't make the pilgrimage with her husband and the rest of the family. Later on young Samuel learned that his mother had planned to take him to the temple and give him to the Lord as soon as she had weaned him.

When she had weaned Samuel, given in answer to prayer, Hannah and Elkanah, who agreed with her commitment, kept their promise. They made ready three bullocks, one ephah of flour, and a bottle of wine, and headed for Shiloh to present Samuel to the Lord.

Since his parents had dedicated him to the Lord all the years of his life, and even before he was born, it fell Samuel's lot to remain at the temple with Eli. There Samuel would prepare for his service to the Lord. Eli the high priest had two sons who were not good examples for a young man who was being brought up for the ministry of the Lord. But Eli was helpful and kind to Samuel. Perhaps Eli had failed to dedicate his boys to the Lord, in contrast to what Hannah and Elkanah had done with Samuel. Had he done so, they might have ended up better. Although Eli was the high priest of God, his sons didn't know the Lord and couldn't have cared less.

Being a child under his care, young Samuel ministered in the temple. Every year the lad looked forward to the visit of his parents on their pilgrimage. Along with her, Samuel's mother brought a little coat that she had made for Samuel with her own hands. Because of the blessings of God upon him and the help of Eli the priest, the boy was able to grow and develop pleasingly in the sight of God and in the eyes of the people.

It broke Samuel's heart time after time as he listened to Eli receiving complaint after complaint from those who came to worship. They complained that Eli's sons, Hophni and Phinehas, were worthless scoundrels, thieves, and extortioners.

While Hophni and Phinehas performed their duties as priests, they would force the worshipers who were sacrificing animals to give them large portions of the meat. It was a known fact that Eli's sons lived in sexual immorality. Eli lost control over his two sons. They completely ignored his fatherly advice.

One night, as the lights before the altar burned dim, young Samuel heard his name being softly called. Thinking for certain that his master, Eli, had summoned him, he hurried to answer. But Eli sent Samuel back to bed. No sooner had he returned to his couch than he heard the same voice again.

Taking no chances, the lad rushed back to Eli's tent, which was nearby, but Eli denied that he had called Samuel. Once again, Samuel went back to bed, but the third time the voice called, "Samuel!" After relating the strange third call to Eli, Samuel was told that it must be the Lord calling.

Back to bed Samuel went. And before he could fall asleep, the call came for the fourth time. "Samuel!" Having been prepared by Eli, Samuel answered, "Speak; for thy servant heareth."

Samuel's first and most difficult assignment from the Lord arrived that night. God's message to him was to be delivered to Eli, and of all people to inform Eli, Samuel felt that he should have been the last. The two had been so very close, and Eli had treated Samuel more like a son. Yet, God had a message to be delivered, a message that would cause "both the ears of every one that heareth it" to "tingle."

Because Eli's sons had made themselves vile and their father had not restrained them, God was going to judge the house of Eli forever. Young Samuel was to inform Eli that he could not in his lifetime offer enough sacrifices to purge the sins of his house. He was finished—poor fellow—and Samuel had to break the news. What a task!

Eli made it less difficult than Samuel thought it would be. Samuel waited until morning and after he had opened the temple doors. Then Eli called to Samuel, "Son, tell me all. Hide nothing from me." So, Samuel related all that the Lord had spoken. Eli, being the servant of the Lord he was, took it well. He said, "It is the Lord; let him do what seemeth good to him."

The Lord was with Samuel, and the people were pleased. This is what is meant by the expression, "and did let none of his words fall to the ground."

Samuel later learned that God had not spoken directly to any other man since the days of Joshua. It was an amazing experience to have the Lord reestablish this oral relationship—with a lad.

Eli could not have been too surprised at the message of the Lord, for he had been forewarned earlier that his two sons would both die the same day. He also knew how corrupt they were. Their sins plagued him night and day.

Samuel's era was a day of weak and fearful men. The crepe was hanging black and deep upon the people's souls. Things looked bad, but God had sent the prophet, Samuel, on the scene to change the climate. His work was cut out for him.

A time of opportunity for a leader had never been better. Samuel knew the conditions as they were. It was no period for drooping heads or limp arms. It was a day for strengthening feeble knees.

The ark of the covenant had fallen into the hands of the Philistines. The ark of the covenant was Israel's symbol of the presence of God–the hands of the Philistines were no place for it. It was not an easy task, but the prophet determined to rescue the ark of the covenant from its twenty-year resting place. To do this was an indication that Samuel was calling the nation back to God.

This called for a reformation, but one had already begun in his heart. It had to start somewhere. He was the one who heard God's voice. He had seen the vision–therefore, he was the man to alter the climate. With the help of the Lord, he did.

The young prophet Samuel would be the champion. God provided the worthy cause. The people would rally, when challenged to do so.

Never could Samuel get away from the watchword Eli, his tutor, had given him, "Speak, Lord, for thy servant heareth." Samuel spent considerable time listening to the Lord and the rest of it trying to do what the Lord said. Much of his success for the Lord, Samuel attributed to being a good listener. This practice linked him up with the invisible treasures of heaven.

Samuel early learned that to be able to do God's work and do it well, one must keep fellowship with Him. This is done by praying and listening. It is by this same method that power for the task becomes available. Samuel had to condition the minds of the Israelites that victory for God's people does not lie in their armies, but in their God. Their attitude toward God had to be changed. Samuel placed a stone at Mizpeh, indicating that victory comes only when people's hearts are right with God.

He refused to allow the people to put their trust in him, a mere man. It was God whom Samuel wanted them to trust. The news spread across the land like wildfire that Samuel would be the Lord's spokesman to replace Eli. The people were thrilled that God had spoken once more to his people. When Hannah, his dedicated mother, heard the news, she was overcome with joy. She had lived in the mountains of Ephraim without her son all of those years.

Every night, God turned from Eli to Samuel when He wanted to speak to His people—God spoke his message through Samuel, who then passed it on to the people.

Since Eli had meant so much to young Samuel, Samuel felt that he could return the favor to other young men coming along. This he did. Although Eli failed his own boys, he was a stay to Samuel. He helped shape Samuel's life for the service of the Lord.

It could have been Eli's devotion to Samuel that attracted him to young Saul and David. So, when the occasion presented itself, Samuel gladly gave them a lift.

It was a blow to Samuel, as he grew older and began to slow down, that the people whom he had served so long began to clamor for a king. Not willing to wait to be forced to step aside, the prophet willingly complied with their request. The Lord had been so gracious to him, and the people had followed so well that he could not resist the request.

In a sense, Israel's clamoring for a king gave Samuel the clue that he was no longer adequate to lead them. They had decided to ask for a new leader of Israel. Most of his remaining days he spent in an effort to help the young king succeed in the reign the Lord had placed upon him.

Samuel's career, coming to an end, brought a close to the service of fifteen judges of Israel who had directed the people. During his many years of leadership, Samuel had kept peace with the foes of Israel. Samuel was not a man of war, like Gideon or Jephthah. He was a man of peace. The people followed well, and even though the Philistines were still strong, and they held sway over some parts of Israel near the border, there was no war.

When the people demanded it, God gave them a king. This ended the long period of the judges. Samuel had been something no other Israelite had been—*prophet, priest, and judge.*

LESSONS FROM SAMUEL

Sharon: I would like to pay tribute to Samuel's good mother. It was in answer to her prayer that God blessed her with that child.

Nell: Sharon is right, and his mother, Hannah, was so conscious that her child was a gift from God in answer to prayer that she dedicated him back to the Lord. This, to me, is the beautiful part of this story.

Jack: Both Nell and Sharon are right, but shouldn't we give Eli some credit for his influence on Samuel?

Becky: There's no doubt about the good influence Eli, the priest, had on young Samuel. But when I think of his good influence on another person's kid, I wonder why he couldn't do something with his own. It almost cancels the good he did for Hannah's son, when I realize what he didn't do with his own. It's a shame and a disgrace the way his kids turned out, and the Bible says, "He restrained them not."

Tom: Becky spoke my feelings. I have always heard that children left to themselves will finally destroy themselves. This happened to the sons of Eli.

Lucy: I have always heard that to "spare the rod will spoil the child." Too often we see the same thing happen today. Most likely, Eli kept so busy working for the Lord, looking after the congregation and working with young prophets like Samuel, that he neglected his own family. Sometimes pastors and other Christian workers give their lives to the people and neglect their own family. This seems to be what Eli did.

Wallie: No doubt God expects his leaders to serve the people, but not to the neglect of their own families. They have an obligation to their homes as well. I think Eli is a good example of this common tragedy, and those who neglect their own family have no excuse for it. By doing so, Eli forfeited his reign to the priesthood. I know some preachers who need to get this lesson from Eli before it's too late.

Tracy: This surely has taught me a lesson. If God ever gives me a family, I'm going to remember the tragic mistake of Eli.

Pastor: The main character in our study is Samuel. However, our discussion has turned on Eli. This can be helpful. He should really teach parents, especially spiritual leaders *how not to do it.* Let's move on to Samuel. He is the mirror we wanted to look into to see ourselves at this time. Who has a good idea for us?

Wallace: Pastor, if any one in the group doubts that God really calls his servants into the ministry, this should settle the question. Not everyone has the same experience in the call, but God calls preachers. Samuel's call was a beautiful experience.

Ed: One of the greatest blessings that I have received from this study of Samuel is that he spent a great deal of his time listening to the Lord. Then he spent the rest of it doing the will of the Lord. I'm going to remember this in my life. My temptation has been to spend too much of my time telling the Lord what I wanted him to do. I have resolved to spend more time listening. With Samuel, I'm going to say, "Speak, Lord, for thy servant heareth."

Lyle: Pastor, Samuel was a champion of a great cause. The people believed in him: therefore, they followed him.

Ed: At present I'm a long way from retirement, but, Samuel is sure to have a good influence on me when I come to it. Still going strong and so far as we know physically fit, Samuel was ready to step down when the people got ready for another leader. He accepted retirement with grace.

Pastor: To conclude with the word "commitment" would even be inadequate to describe the reason for the great leader, Samuel. With the dedication of a Samuel, God can take and successfully use any and every one of us. How much of Samuel can you see in yourself? What is there about him that you would like to emulate? We can't all be Samuel's, but we can all be what God wants us to be with his help.

To get the most personal benefit from this character study, take a pencil and a sheet of paper and answer the following questions.

1. What were the strong points or characteristics of the character? List them on paper.

2. What were the weaknesses of this character? List them.

3. What did the character have going for him or her? List the things in his favor.

4. What decisions or choices did the character make that you think were wrong? List the wrong ones, then list the right ones.

5. How can you benefit by your study of this character?

6. Have you really been face to face with yourself?

Notes:

9
Dumber than a Donkey
(Balaam)
Numbers 22:5-24:25; 31:8

Too many people, like Balaam, want to die the death of the righteous. Like Balaam, though, they are not willing to pay the price to do so.

Balaam made his own choice while asking God, "Let me die the death of the righteous, and let my last end be like his!" (Numbers 23:10). He lived his life contrary to what he was asking. It was really Balaam's fault that his life ended as it did, rather than as he prayed it would.

Our character was actually a marvelous man. He could pray a convincing prayer. He was an astute actor. But he professed one thing while possessing another. His life was a series of inconsistencies. His days were choked with contradictions.

Balaam was such a "modern man" that he could be found in every congregation today. As we thoroughly study him, we find a "wee bit" of ourselves in him. Yes, we can see some of the man in us.

At times the prophet towers like a giant, while at others, he is less than a pygmy. There was a period when the prophet's reputation soared so high that it was said of him, "He whom thou blessest is best, and he whom thou cursest is cursed" (Numbers 22:6).

Poor fellow Balaam, like too many others he had his price even though he made his boast: "If Balak would give me his house full of silver and gold, I cannot go beyond the word of the Lord my God, to do less or more" (Numbers 22:18).

At such moments, one could adore and almost worship Balaam.

Remembering the scriptural adage, "Let him that thinketh he standeth take heed lest he fall," I would have warned him. "Balaam, be careful—the devil will try you." And the devil did.

His further words to the princes, whom Balak had sent laden with gifts, were: "Tarry ye also here this night, that I might know what the Lord will say unto me more" (Num. 22:18). You can see that perhaps he did have his price. At least Satan was on his trail. Would the big man stumble?

Balaam knew the will of God, for God had given it to him in plain, simple language. But Balaam was on the verge of compromise. He was beginning not to sound like the same Balaam who prayed, "Let me die the death of the righteous, and let my last end be like his!"

Nor was he sounding like the same prophet who stood on the hilltop of Moab and prophesied: "I shall see him, but not now: I shall behold him, but not nigh there shall come a Star out of Jacob, and a Sceptre shall rise out of Israel" (Num. 24:17). Imagine it. Balaam issued this famous prophecy concerning none other than Jesus Christ, the coming Messiah of Israel!

But Balak, king of Moab, didn't take no for an answer. Satan never stops pressing his battle. The higher the price offered, the weaker Balaam became.

Thinking he couldn't make God change his mind, Balaam asked the messenger to stay another night. Balaam, of course, "wanted to sleep on it." Rather than changing God's mind, Balaam was growing weaker and weaker. His feet were on slippery glass. He had more than he could stand. In his weakness for honor and the love of gold, Balaam sold out, instead of standing true to the light God gave him.

When you have a question about an activity, attitude, or thought, remember that there may be wrong in it. Let it alone. When conviction raises a question, simply don't follow through on the questionable. So often, people try to gain approval by saying, "There's nothing wrong with it, is there?" The safe stance is to put the borderline cases in the forbidden category.

The moment Balaam began to stifle his convictions, that

moment he began to commit soul suicide. When he began to follow his own whims and fancies and turned a deaf ear to the will of God, Balaam had "cleared" his own conscience, having deadened it to the voice of God.

Reportedly, somewhere in South America there is a flower known as the "sensitive plant." At the first touch of the finger, this plant begins to close its petals. If touched enough, the sensitive plant closes completely—it can be touched to death! Man's conscience is like that! It is sensitive at first, but it can be soothed, coaxed, and confused. It becomes deadened and no longer accuses you. This happened to the compromising Balaam.

The sad hour came when the angel of Jehovah, standing with drawn sword in the path of the prophet, didn't even recognize him as Balaam. Balaam had fallen for ill-gotten gains, "filthy lucre." Who could forget the story of the ass on which Balaam rode when confronted by the angel of the Lord? (Num. 22: 27-30). It was a tragedy when a dumb ass could see and hear what the man of God, because of sin, could not see and hear.

Like a weakened Samson, Balaam had gone too far to turn back. Before he realized it, he had played into the hands of Satan.

Disloyalty to God and his will causes men like Balaam to forfeit their sincere heart's desire to "die the death of the righteous." Instead, he died with the enemies of God.

Listen to Balaam's death notice and mark well those with whom he died. "And they slew the kings of Midian, beside the rest of them that were slain; namely, Evi, and Rekem, and Zur, and Hur, and Reba, five kings of Midian: Balaam also the son of Beor they slew with the sword" (Num. 31:8). What a horribly tragic ending to his story.

Ambition is good, but not good enough. Heavenly aspiration is noble, but a person can aspire and still meet God unprepared. How could Balaam, with so much going for him, come to such a tragic end?

What happened to the man who got off to such a good start? He goes down in history as a false prophet. Peter refers to

Balaam's madness. Jude wrote about the "error of Balaam." Even John the apostle spoke about the "doctrine of Balaam," because it had the curse of God upon it.

TRY THIS ON FOR SIZE

Now that you have read this chapter, take a look at yourself. Better now than too late.

In the light of what Balaam became, over against what he could have become, size up yourself.

Stand before this full-size mirror for a good look. You may have all the potential this character had. You may not have all going for you that he had, but you must, and you will, decide your outcome.

As he did, you may wish to die the death of the righteous. If so, you had better determine the direction your life must take to do so and do it.

Patty: Pastor, the Bible doesn't say much about Balaam, but what it says surely does hit home to most of us. All too often, we desire things we aren't willing to pay the price for. It is one thing to want; it is altogether another thing to do. Many of us want or desire something on our own terms. Desired achievement comes at a price. One unwilling to pay the price is unworthy of the achievement. This was Balaam's case. I wonder if some of us aren't guilty at times.

Steve: We don't become followers of Christ Jesus on our own terms. He made this very clear, when he said "If any man would come after me, let him deny himself, take up his cross daily, and follow me."

Bill: Compromise is one of Satan's most effective tools. If he can't get us to go all the way, he will take us as far as he can. He searches for our weak spots, and if we allow him to do so, he will invade where our defense is weakest. For this reason, we should walk daily with the Lord and depend on him to be our help against the enemy.

Pastor: Dick, from the expression on your face you must have a word for the group.

Dick: Yes, pastor, I have been reminded that temptation to compromise is one of the biggest problems of people both young and old. The devil doesn't mind if we are religious, just so we don't get too excited and involved in it. He doesn't mind if we go to church on Sunday, so long as we cooperate with him the rest of the week.

Bruce: Dick's right. Balaam knew what was right; he also knew that God was not going to change His mind, but as he looked at the princes of Balak loaded with gifts–which turned out to be Balaam's price–he was too weak to refuse the offer. Rather than abiding by what he knew to be right, Balaam, in the process of hardening his conscience, said to the visitor: "Tarry ye here this night that I might know the word of the Lord concerning the matter." He knew the will of the Lord, but by morning it would be easier for him to disobey the Lord and sell out to Satan.

Dave: When it was announced that our Bible study would be on Balaam, I gave a big yawn. I had no idea so many lessons could be picked up from a Bible character so little known. I've learned that he was like many of us.

Bob: This is somewhat a repeat, but as long as the tempter can keep us considering his proposition, he draws us nearer and nearer to a compromise. Blinded by his concern for dirty money the man who was supposed to be God's servant did not even recognize the angel of Jehovah who headed him off in the middle of the road. It took the dumb donkey to recognize the angel of the Lord, on behalf of the more-than-dumb prophet.

Pastor: Let a person begin to stifle his convictions and before he can realize it, he has committed soul suicide. Balaam is a good example of a man who went down in defeat, even though he had so much going for him.

Never engage in a conversation with Satan. He will seduce you. He will overpower you.

If you tend toward a proud mind and a haughty spirit, conquer them, or they will overcome you.

Take a look at yourself and any kinship you find to Balaam or any tendencies you saw in him that seem to lurk in you. Call upon the Holy Spirit to help you subdue them.

The same tendencies that at first had no power over Balaam, but finally wrecked him, can do the same for you if yielded to in any degree.

Let me assure you that in Jesus Christ only, we have the power to carry out our desires, not only to live the life of the righteous, but after having done so, we will die the death of the righteous. The decision is yours and mine. We only can make this decision.

Don't forget the man who desired to die the death of the righteous but missed it. Instead the Bible said: "Balaam also the son of Beor they slew with the sword." Against his better judgment, Balaam planned his life that way. What a pity!

SPIRITUAL THERAPY

To get the most personal benefit from this character study, take a pencil and a sheet of paper and answer the following questions.

1. What were the strong points or characteristics of the character? List them on paper.

2. What were the weaknesses of this character? List them.

3. What did the character have going for him or her? List the things in his favor.

4. What decisions or choices did the character make that you think were wrong? List the wrong ones, then list the right ones.

5. How can you benefit by your study of this character?

6. Have you really been face to face with yourself?

Notes:

10
A Drink of Living Water
(The Woman at the Well)
John 4:5-30

A woman of Samaria approached Jacob's well at noon, in the heat of the day. She did it to avoid contact with the "nicer" ladies of the city, who drew their water either early or late in the day.

She was sick and tired of the sinful life she was living, yet ignorant of how to live a better one. Rather than face the good women of the city at the well, she would rather have suffered without the water. She felt safer going for water in the middle of the day, in spite of the blistering Middle Eastern sun. She would rather suffer heat than to face ridicule and criticism that known sinners received from their neighbors. True, she was considered a "woman of ill repute" by those around her.

So, she had come with her water pot for her daily supply of water. Unlike other times when she had sneaked along the path to the well and back, this trip was vastly different. To her surprise, there sat a thirsty man on the curb of the well. As she drew nearer—to her further amazement—she discovered that the man was a Jew.

Not only was this woman of bad reputation amazed that the man on the curb of the well was a Jew, she was astonished that he, a Jew, was in Samaria at all. As the usual course, Jews bypassed the country of the Samaritans, for these people had no dealings with each other.

Pretending that she had not seen the man, with her eyes gazing downward, the woman let her bucket to the bottom of the well and pulled it up filled with fresh water.

This earthy woman was not easily shocked—but something happened that almost shocked her out of her sandals, if she were wearing sandals. This young Jew made a request of her. The Samaritan woman was not surprised that the poor man was thirsty—but she was flabbergasted that a Jew would make a request of her, or even speak to her, for that matter. "Self-respecting" Jews just didn't do such things!

The Jewish man's manner was unusual, because his request for water was gentle and persuasive. There was nothing dictatorial or dogmatic in his request. It was simply, "Give me to drink." The woman hardly knew how to respond. Jews and Samaritans never spoke to one another, because of deep-seated prejudices going back almost 800 years. Yet, this man spoke so freely and gently.

The woman frankly asked why the young man was being so personal with her. This man was different—he was gentle, kind, and even *loving.* She had known many men, and most of them had equated love with lust. But not this man, surely.

This man talked about "living water." This puzzled her to no end—water that would quench her thirst forever. She would never again have to draw water from the well! The very imagination of that piqued her interest. Coming to the well every day—and especially in the sweltering heat—was no little chore. She was willing to find out about this "living water" if it meant not coming back to draw from the well.

If Jacob's well contained such water, why—this Jewish man had neither a rope nor a bucket! How could he possibly produce such water? Jacob had done well to leave this source of water to his posterity. How could this young man offer any better?

Sitting right there on the curb of the well, this Jewish stranger began to explain the difference in the two waters. By this time, this much-married woman, feeling more relaxed in his presence, was interested in knowing more concerning the water about which the man spoke. The thoughts of not ever being thirsty again, and not having to slip out to draw water, and not being afraid of the women of the city anymore—these thoughts grabbed her. This woman had now become concerned about having the gift of living water.

Growing bolder by the minute, the Samaritan woman asked for that living water, only to receive an astonishing response. The young Jew requested that she rush back into the city and bring her husband, as though he, too, might receive this water. Quite shocked at such a request, but feeling that she must be truthful, she told him that she had no husband.

This young man replied, "Yes, you have had five husbands, and the man you are now living with is not your husband." This young man, Jesus, read her life like an open book. The woman was stunned that he knew all about her morbid character. She indicated, too, that she looked for a Messiah who would come and solve their problems.

It was then that Jesus revealed to the woman of Samaria that she was talking to that Messiah in person.

So excited and elated was she that she forgot the water from Jacob's well. She left her water pot and ran back into the city to tell her former men friends and others that she had found the Messiah.

As she arrived in the city, her joy was superabundant. She now had such a power and convincing testimony that she emptied the entire city of Sychar. She wanted every resident to meet this man this unusual man who had told her everything that she had ever done, this man who had given her that "water that springs up into everlasting life."

The excitement, along with the evident, drastic changes in the woman's life, was so convincing to the entire town that Sychar became a ghost city overnight while its inhabitants went outside the city to see this man for themselves. Many believed because of the woman's testimony, but even more believed on him because they were led out to see him for themselves.

The Bible injunction, "the Son of man is come to seek and to save that which is lost," was never truer than as demonstrated in the case of the woman at the well.

We can never lose sight of the fact that Christ came into the world to save sinners—even the chief of sinners, one like this woman.

LESSONS FROM THE WOMAN AT THE WELL

Jesus' attitude toward Samaria and the people who lived there should be a reminder to us that "God is no respecter of persons." Knowing this, we should cultivate a love for all people.

Had Jesus been a bigot, like some people, he would have bypassed Samaria. This woman would not have been saved, and neither would others in the city. Many in the city believed on Jesus as the Messiah because of the woman's testimony and changed life. They never would have been introduced to Jesus, of course, if Jesus had stayed clear of Samaria and the Samaritans.

When we become as concerned for people—all people, any people—as Jesus was, we "must needs go through Samaria," too.

Another thought—when we are saved, somewhere along the line, we will want to share it.

The extent or depth to which people have gone into sin makes no difference—if they genuinely repent and ask for God's forgiveness, he will forgive them and save them from the "guttermost to the uttermost."

It should not become necessary for God to give a second chance to those who need it and want it on God's terms. But the gospel is just that. God offers another chance—often, many chances.

Forgiven of their sins, persons should lose no time before they share their faith with others who need a similar experience of forgiveness. The woman of Sychar is a prime example.

If genuine, and not put under a bushel, a Christian experience such as this woman had will influence others for Christ.

Professed Christianity that has no positive influence on others could be plastic or phony. We should all examine our relationship to Jesus Christ.

Every Christian life should be so lived that others could see our good works, and glorify our Father in heaven. When the people in Sychar saw this woman's transformed life, they became convinced. She was changed, and her life spoke for itself.

FACE TO FACE . . . WITH YOURSELF

Before we leave the woman at the well, let's get before the mirror.

We should investigate our hearts for critical attitudes toward others—perhaps others who have lived sinful lives or others who are "different" from us. What was it in the lives of the Samaritans which drove the woman to draw her water at noon? Do we tend to frown on others when they have fallen into sin?

Jesus loves no one's sins—yet, he loves all sinners. Paul declared, "I am become all things to all men, that I might by all means save some" (1 Cor. 9:22). We can never win people to faith in Christ until we can evidence our concern in them.

Others may take their stand with the hungry disciples who returned with their food purchase and couldn't understand Jesus' concern for this sinner. Among us are those who desire to see sinners saved, yet are interested only in "the more respectable sinners" joining their fellowship.

Still others of us should examine our experience with Christ to see if it is genuine, and if so, why we don't rush to our friends and neighbors and share our faith with them? We may not attract the entire town, but there are people that we can influence for Christ. The fruit of a Christian is another Christian.

SPIRITUAL THERAPY

To get the most personal benefit from this character study, take a pencil and a sheet of paper and answer the following questions.

1. What were the strong points or characteristics of the character? List them on paper.

2. What were the weaknesses of this character? List them.

3. What did the character have going for him or her? List the things in his favor.

4. What decisions or choices did the character make that you think were wrong? List the wrong ones, then list the right ones.

5. How can you benefit by your study of this character?

6. Have you really been face to face with yourself?

Notes:

11
The King of Traitors
(Judas)
Matthew 26:24; Luke 22:3-4; John 6:70, 13:21-30

Brutus who plotted against and helped murder Julius Caesar . . .
Benedict Arnold who turned against his own revolutionaries . . .
Quisling who sold out Norway to the Nazis . . .

The mention of these names causes bad vibrations. They were traitors, "turncoats," men who betrayed their country, their convictions, and their publicly-espoused causes.

But the name that is most synonymous with "traitor" is *Judas Iscariot!* Of all people who came in contact with Jesus, Judas presents the saddest case. It is truly scriptural that it would have been far better for him if he had never been born (Matt. 26:24).

Jesus loved him, just as he loved vacillating Simon Peter and the other imperfect disciples. Judas had enjoyed the same privileges and opportunities that they had. While Simon Peter turned away from his sinful blunders and became a rock, Judas turned his back on Jesus and became a tool in the hands of Satan.

Yes, "all have sinned, and come short of the glory of God." But of all sinners ever born, Judas must rank as the chief of them all. His actions and life should serve as a perpetual warning to everyone who hears his story—and everyone should hear it. You could never have known certain parts of it, if he himself had not told it.

As an apostle, Judas was admitted to the highest and holiest that Jesus had to offer. He was taken into the little family of men with whom Jesus spent most of his time during his three years of earthly ministry. He was one of those with whom Jesus was intimately conversant. Where Jesus went, Judas was welcomed with him. He did not have to dine with the servants, but he drank of the same cup with Jesus, and in all respects fared as Jesus fared. Judas ate the miraculous bread with Jesus, when the loaves and fishes were multiplied. He also ate the Passover with the Master. Judas stood alongside of John, and Peter, and James. So trusted was Judas that he was the treasurer of the group. Imagine it. He kept the money bags.

He was one of The Twelve, those who had the closest fellowship with Jesus. To think that he heard the gracious teachings of the Lord day by day. He literally "sat in heavenly places" on earth with Christ Jesus.

Judas was highly esteemed by the little group. His ability and energy for business activities didn't go unnoticed, for when the group began to accumulate funds, they saw in Judas the ability of capable management. They selected him as their treasurer. Not even once had he given them reason to doubt his honesty, for men are not likely to trust their money to one whom they suspect of being a thief. Certainly they did not select as chancellor of the exchequer one whose honesty was in question. Nor does it seem that the majority of the apostles ever suspected him, even at the very last of Jesus' public ministry. When Jesus told them that he was about to be betrayed by one of them, they began to reply, "Lord, is it I?"

Judas' imposing personality and good educational qualities–probably the best educated one in the group–gave him prestige among the disciples, and it put him in line for getting closer and closer to Jesus. He was suave, smooth, and cunning.

On top of all this, for three years he was given the opportunity to perform the preparatory work of an apostle. He was drilled in religious facts and was able to study Christ day by day. His life had every uplifting influence and every heavenward advantage. Yet, he refused to follow the light from above. Instead, he listened to the voice of sin-cursed ambition and as a result, he was swept down into eternal doom.

Jesus permitted Judas to have the same things as the other disciples. During his public ministry, Jesus allowed Judas to be with him, to witness his miracles, to listen to his instructions, and to behold the greatness of his character. At the Passover supper, Jesus stooped down and washed Judas' feet, just as he did those of the other apostles.

When The Twelve were sent out two by two, Judas was with them. And he was given the power of casting out demons and healing diseases. Like the rest, he seemed to have been successful on his mission. You have to admit that Judas had some good, admirable qualities that led to his admission to the apostolic group.

To realize fully the possibilities Judas had, one must recognize that Judas, like all other men, had free will, an ability to choose. The Scriptures make plain the fact that God has made men with the freedom to choose. "They have no choice but to choose." God forces no one to accept or reject him.

It is true that the Old Testament prophesied that one would betray Jesus, but nowhere did it indicate that Judas was to be the man. It was left open to the free will of man. It could have been one of the other apostles. Judas was a rational, choosing person—and even though he fulfilled the prophecy, he was responsible for his choice in betraying Jesus. Prophecy does not destroy responsibility. Men are free in going to their doom.

Not one time during the public ministry of Jesus did he make any public disclosure of Judas. Several times Jesus made statements that appeared to be a warning to Judas, a warning for him to change his ways. When Jesus spoke such words, they were as applicable to any other one of The Twelve as they were to him. He always spared Judas the pains and the disgrace of an exposure.

Judas' rejection of Jesus was a process and not one act. This process came to a climax on the night of the Last Supper, when the devil took complete possession of Judas, and led him out to betray the Master.

It seemed that all of the apostles were expecting Jesus to set up a temporal kingdom here on earth. Even more, Judas looked for that, for he carried the money bag. He yearned for the day when he would be the secretary of the treasury in King Jesus' Kingdom. What visions of grandeur he had. He expected Jesus to head up this kingdom after conquering the Roman Empire.

Becoming disillusioned because Jesus was slow to take action, Judas found himself growing impatient and out of sympathy with his Master and his method of doing things. Judas became harder and became embittered by disappointment in Jesus' not going on and setting up his kingdom.

Many theories have been advanced as to why Judas betrayed Jesus. But all such theories aim at justifying him, and thus legitimatizing the Lord's election of him to the apostleship. All such theories are mere fancies.

They are not only unsupported, but directly discounted by the Gospels. According to John, Jesus said, "Have not I chosen you twelve, and one of you is a devil?" (John 6:70). And Luke reported: "Then Satan entered into Judas surnamed Iscariot, being of the number of the twelve. And he went his way, and communed with the chief priests and captains, how he might betray him unto them" (Luke 22:3-4).

The Gospel writers present the betrayal as a diabolical crime. That someone would betray Jesus into the hands of sinners was somehow in the eternal purpose, and in the determinate will and foreknowledge of God. God chose Judas as one of The Twelve, but not for one minute are we to assume that God chose him to betray Jesus. Jesus saw in Judas at the outset the possibility of greater and higher things. Instead of accomplishing the greater things of life, Judas yielded to Satan and to the baser impulses of his sinful nature.

Day by day he let those sins conquer him by degrees, and finally they had complete control over him. When he reached the low point of the process it was Passover week. Judas came to feel that his hopes were dashed–he would not reach what he expected, a post in Jesus' cabinet in the Kingdom. During that fateful Passover Week, Judas decided to abandon the whole cause and to carry with him what poor spoils he could collect. Why, hadn't he sacrificed to follow Jesus? Hadn't he done without?

Now was the time to cash in. Before Judas realized what he had done, he had become a self-deceived pietist. He knew good and approved good, though he did not consciously practice it in his life—for he was a slave to Satan and to his own low desires and selfish passions.

Step by step, Judas had plunged to the depths—until he reached the bottom. He had turned down countless opportunities. He had surrendered to his hellish sins, only to finish his journey and go to an endless hell. While Peter was out weeping and repenting of his sins, Judas was out hanging himself. Repentance leads to a promising future, while Judas' remorse and desperate actions led him nowhere but to moral ruin.

In order to give Judas plenty of time to recover himself, Jesus foretold the fact that one of The Twelve would betray him. Although the event followed according to the prediction, Judas was not foreordained to this sin by any fatal necessity. Thus, Jesus gave him warning and opportunity to recover, if he wanted to, from the snare of the devil.

He was not forced to betray Jesus, but to the contrary, all the influences of association with Christ would tend to keep Judas from doing it. Satan, though, gradually gained entrance into Judas' heart, and when he did, Judas was a willing instrument in his devilish hands.

It touched Jesus in a tender spot to think that one of his closest men would turn traitor, after enjoying distinguished favors from Him. How could any person carry out this tragedy after Jesus warned him? Why didn't Judas turn from his hell-bent course? It was Judas' to choose what he wanted to do. Jesus never forced anyone to follow him, but he gave the opportunity, and Judas rejected it.

At the Last Supper the climax had come, and the devil took charge of Judas—not to make him melancholy, not to drive him distracted, but to possess him with a prejudice against Christ and his teachings. The devil excited Judas to a covetous desire for the wages of unrighteousness.

You must not lose sight of the truth that the devil was in Judas before that ill-fated night. All along he had succeeded in getting Judas to yield to his will. Now the devil had reached the point where he had Judas trapped. No longer could Judas resist, and the devil assumed complete charge of his life. Judas' purpose to betray Jesus had ripened into a fixed resolution. He was putty in the hands of evil. The germs of sin that had been gradually unfolding in him were then turned loose, full grown.

At the Last Supper, Jesus knew what was in Judas' heart. Jesus turned to the disciples and said, "Verily, verily, I say unto you, that one of you shall betray me" (John 13:21). The disciples were shocked and began looking at one another quizzically. Jesus said, "The one to whom I give a sop will betray me." Jesus gave the piece of bread to Judas, but the disciples surmised that Jesus had sent Judas out on a business errand. Even then they did not suspect.

Jesus said to Judas, "That thou doest, do quickly" (John 13:27). Jesus was not directing Judas to sin. Jesus, in essence, was indicating: "Judas, if you are determined to go through with this crime and sin, do it. Do it swiftly. Do it now. Get it over with." Judas did everything by his own free choice.

To this day, the name Judas calls to mind the chilling word, "traitor"!

CHARACTER ANALYSIS OF JUDAS

Pastor: The Bible reveals the bad, as well as the good, of the people it features. Of course, more bad than good is mentioned in the character before us. Earlier in this session Jake had a question concerning Judas. Since we are now ready to make an analysis of the man, Jake, repeat your question.
Jake: Why did Judas do such a horrible thing, and for such a pitiful price?
Danny: Let me answer that. As we searched the Bible about Judas, I came to the conclusion that Judas had played along into the hands of Satan so long that when the final decision had to be made, he had gone too far. It had become impossible to turn

back. Satan had him in his clutches. And when the showdown came, the High Priest would give Judas only thirty pieces of silver to close the deal. Judas' selfish ambition weighed heavily in his decision. So, at the last minute, Judas salvaged what he could. Added to this character's weakness for whatever he could get, he had little by little yielded to the control of Satan, until at last he had no power to turn back.

Bill: It's a good idea, in the light of what Judas did, to fully decide never to compromise with Satan. You just can't win over him—going it alone by yourself. He'll mess you up.

Jerry: Yes, I was thinking how so many people allow the spirit of covetousness to master them. As we all know, the Bible says, "The love of money is the root of all evil."

Janell: In the light of Judas' decision, do others of you have some advice for the rest of us?

Gail: Yes, even though Judas had gotten into the fellowship of the redeemed, and though he performed as an apostle, all the while he was letting Satan take complete control of his life. The other eleven had no idea that Judas was a devil from the beginning.

Frank: According to Judas' life, it is possible that some of us could actually be living a lie. I hope not, but it's conceivable. Only time will tell. For this very reason, I think each of us should personally examine his relationship to Jesus Christ. There is no place for plastic people. It is too serious a matter.

Pastor: Thanks, Frank and Gail. Judas should be a lesson to all of us.

Judy: He surely is. I think Judas' attitude told on him throughout. When Mary anointed Jesus with her perfume, you remember how Judas argued that the price of the perfume should be applied to help for the poor. I really doubt if he meant that. Anyway, I began to be leery of his character. I don't see how he could have displayed that selfish spirit. It wouldn't surprise me what Judas would do. If you caught the "dig" that Jesus gave Judas, you could see that Jesus had evidently given up on the man. Having freedom of choice, and allowed to make up his mind,

Judas had let Satan help him make it up.

Hal: In this study, I noticed, too, that Judas seemed to be jealous of James and John, as well as Simon Peter. Of course, all of his decisions, stemming from a selfish, jealous attitude, would tend to be in Satan's favor, even though they were hurtful to Judas.

Jim: It's with mixed emotions that young people make all of their important decisions. This was no less true with Judas. You could sense this when he pretended to love the poor and when he was making a deal for one of the main seats in the Kingdom.

Even when he left the Last Supper to betray Jesus, none of the other disciples suspected anything other than that Judas was running an errand for Jesus.

Dave: After this study of Judas, the man who betrayed his Lord, I can never be the same. For one thing certain, I'll never be part of a gang that pretends to follow Jesus, but doesn't mean it. Of course, Judas couldn't have been a genuine Christian. He was in the company of believers, but he himself was not one. He was a counterfeit from the beginning.

Jerry: I'm sure that all of us would agree that Judas' commitment to Jesus was never real. He made a profession, but didn't have a possession. I wonder why he followed Jesus' call, anyway?

Pastor: As you know, Zealots were common among Palestinian Jews when Judas was growing up. This political and racial movement sought to arouse an insurrection, to throw off the power of Rome, and to restore the Jews to independence and control. Judas saw in Jesus the potential as the leader who could and possibly would do just that. It was more political with Judas than religious. If we knew the whole truth, I believe Judas' purpose in joining the group was more selfish than patriotic.

What Jesus really intended to do was never fully understood by Judas. No doubt his fond ambition was for Jesus to sit upon an earthly throne, and Judas wanted to be "in on the ground floor," certain to reap a reward of position and power.

It is my fervent hope and prayer that none of us profess to be followers of Jesus Christ and not make sure that we have the real thing. Let none of us serve Jesus for selfish gain.

Let me conclude with this word. Judas had every chance and opportunity that the other disciples had. The power of choice was his. He went to his own place. He didn't have to do what he did. His destiny was one of his own choosing. The devil may tempt, but he can't force. We make our own decisions. Let's let Judas be a constant warning to us, everytime we make a choice.

Like Judas, we are responsible for our decisions and actions. Judas is an example of a life of pretense, sham, and hypocrisy. His betrayal of Jesus came over a period of time. In the beginning he probably didn't intend to do what he finally did. He fell into the snares of the devil by not plotting a superior course.

Had Judas been a genuine disciple, he would have repented like Simon Peter. If so, God would have forgiven him. But he was remorseful and not repentant. Remorse by itself is not sufficient.

LESSONS AND CONCLUSIONS WE LEARN FROM JUDAS

Satan doesn't give up because one joins the fellowship of the redeemed.

It's possible to perform as a saint of God, while all the time Satan is gradually taking possession of your life.

A person may be gradually selling out to Satan, and even his closest companions may not know it.

We may fool the gang, but in time Satan will make a fool out of us, if we let him.

Popularity with the group doesn't guarantee one's final outcome.

A good beginning in life, though helpful, doesn't insure that the ending will be all right.

The greater one's privileges, the greater the responsibility.

Opportunities and privileges don't guarantee character.

Having freedom of choice, each person decides for himself the destiny of his soul.

People in turn choose their master, which in turn fixes their destiny.

No one can be fully to blame for the other fellow's choice. It is for everyone to decide for himself.

Never have a "rap" session with Satan. You can't handle him. You are dealing with "principalities and powers," not flesh and blood.

Satan's purpose is to defeat everyone he can–don't be unaware of his devices.

Jesus offers everyone the rights and benefits of a Christian, but the decision to accept is personal.

Prophecy doesn't destroy personal and individual responsibility of choice. But Satan will help make your choices, if you allow it.

To betray Jesus is a process–not merely one act.

It is too late when one ends up in the snare of Satan. Selfish ambition can lead a person there.

Profession without possession of eternal life leads down a dead end street.

You can't always judge a teacher by the way some of his pupils turn out.

FACE TO FACE . . . WITH YOURSELF

Do you see any of yourself in Judas?

Can you believe that some of Judas could be in you?

Judas had some good points in his life. See how many of them you can recall.

Never for one minute believe that Judas was a victim of circumstance.

Remember that Judas had the same right to freedom of choice that you have.

Before ending this study, write out four decisions concerning your life you have made as a result of studying Judas' life.

SPIRITUAL THERAPY

To get the most personal benefit from this character study, take a pencil and a sheet of paper and answer the following questions.

1. What were the strong points or characteristics of the character? List them on paper.

2. What were the weaknesses of this character? List them.

3. What did the character have going for him or her? List the things in his favor.

4. What decisions or choices did the character make that you think were wrong? List the wrong ones, then list the right ones.

5. How can you benefit by your study of this character?

6. Have you really been face to face with yourself?

Notes:

12
Face to Face . . . with Yourself!
(YOU!)
Proverbs 27:19

What do you think of mirrors? If you are a woman, do you keep one available in your purse? If you are a man, do you have one handy in your room? Are you superstitious about the mishap of breaking a mirror? Do you like mirrors, or do you avoid them?

Every human being is different. Some gravitate to mirrors. Some use mirrors only when absolutely necessary. One man remarked, "I guess the worst thing I have to do is get up in the early morning and look at my mug in the mirror!" Some people are being truthful when they make a statement like that.

Thackeray observed, "The world is a looking glass and gives back to every man the reflection of his own face." Every person must decide what he wants to be and see. No other can make this choice for you.

The people who have made an impact on the world are those who have refused to remain as they were. They determined to live life to its fullest.

History records that Louis Pasteur was only a mediocre student. While he was away in school, his teachers wrote little summary notes to his parents back home. One of his teachers wrote: "He is the smallest boy in the class." Another commented, "Louis is the least brilliant boy in the class." Another remarked, "Louis has made the least progress of anybody in his class this year." His father wondered whether it was worthwhile and worth the cost to keep Louis in school so far away from home.

In his first letter home, Louis wrote, "Just be patient and trust me. I'll do better as I go on." He had determined that he would not remain as he was. He set for himself a challenge, a goal. He made up his mind, though considered a "dullard," that someday he would be and do something worthwhile.

At the age of forty-six, Pasteur suffered a stroke. Dragging himself day after day into his laboratory and forcing himself to painfully gruel over his microscope, he continued his research. We remember his name and his tremendous discoveries, but we are prone to foget his handicaps. With the odds against him, as they were, if Louis Pasteur had not set for himself a controlling purpose in life, he would have been a failure, and we never would have heard of him.

Life can really begin only when you discover yourself. Self-improvement must begin with self-analysis. We must know ourselves. This calls for a course of self-knowledge. Before being willing to come face to face . . . with themselves. They must stare the facts in the face.

A mere glance at oneself is not enough. To be somebody, ambition must be sparked by something. True indeed is the scriptural adage, "As a man thinketh in his heart, so is he." Shakespeare's Macbeth believed in nothing, and as a result, he lived and died for nothing.

Macbeth moaned in futility:

> To-morrow, and to-morrow, and to-morrow,
> Creeps in this petty pace from day to day,
> To the last syllable of recorded time;
> And all our yesterdays have lighted fools
> The way to dusty death.
> Out, out, brief candle!
> Life's but a walking shadow, a poor player
> That struts and frets his hour upon the stage
> And then is heard no more: it is a tale
> Told by an idiot, full of sound and fury,
> Signifying nothing.

If life to you is worth living, you must make it happen. Life doesn't have to happen as it does to some people. You, and they, could make it different.

Your attitude about life counts for more than your heredity, or your environment. When describing his life as being worthwhile, Paul didn't give much credit to his heredity or his environment. Rather, he stated that life to him was what the Lord Jesus Christ meant to him. The fellow that doesn't start somewhere is never apt to get there. An unknown sage said, "You can't correct your faults unless you know them any better than you can come back from someplace you have never been."

Once you have made the discovery, be willing to accept yourself as you are. All too many persons have remained failures because they were not willing to accept themselves as they were, and willing to start from there. They wanted to be like someone else, not realizing that such was impossible.

Often it is the handicapped person that is most victorious in life. Theodore Roosevelt said, "I may be an average man, but I will work at it harder than an average man." Most successful people have at one time or another had one foot off the upward rung of the ladder, and the other almost off.

The person with ten talents and the one with five each doubled his ability by the proper attitude and use of what he had. The man who buried his would no doubt have done the same thing with five or ten, had they been given to him. It was his outlook on life which caused him to bury his talent. It was his attitude toward his master that killed his ambition. Unwilling to accept himself as he was, the poor fellow had no goal to achieve. He had made no plans for self-improvement. The world was no better; in fact, it lost some of its value because the man took more from it than he contributed to it.

Your willingness to face yourself as you are and where you are will determine your hope of ever being the person you could become. Your choice at this point will make or break you. The characters presented in this book will reveal the truth of this statement. Some of them succeeded *in spite of* their limitations.

Others succeeded *because of* their limitations, while some failed, who had no reason to fail.

Every happy and useful life has a basic goal. God has a plan and purpose for every life, and no one else can fill your place. Jesus taught, "to every man his work." This does not mean "to every person some work." Nothing more is expected of an individual than for him to do the best he can with what he has. This is what the Master teaches in the parable of the talents. The right attitude toward what one has is of vital importance. Far more important is it to rightly respect and faithfully use the ability one has than to be highly endowed with talents not used.

YOU, too, must decide the niche that you will fill in this world. Will you just come along for the ride? Will you take life as it comes, and let the world shape you into its mold? Or, will you accept Paul's admonition, "Be not conformed to this world, but be ye transformed"? It's yours to decide. Most likely no one will force it upon you. You will decide for yourself.

Just as God has a plan for everyone, our Lord has a basic purpose for your life. The writer to the Hebrews stated it, "For this cause he is the mediator of the New Testament, that by means of death . . . they which are called might receive the promise of the eternal inheritance." To accomplish his objective, Jesus went to the cross, where he paid the penalty for all our sins.

Without a purpose or a chief aim, Thomas Edison never could have gone from the lonely beginning of a butcher to the leading inventor of the world. The chasm between his lowly birth in a log cabin, in the mountains of Kentucky, and the presidency of the United States of America could never have been bridged by Abraham Lincoln had he not been a man with a consuming definite aim for his life.

Many of us could do much better if, like David, we would "purpose in our hearts" that which would be a worthy, yet an attainable, objective for our lives.

If you have never done so, why not ask yourself a few questions? The Bible says, "If any man will to do his will, he shall know the doctrine, whether it be of God or whether I speak of myself" (John 7:17).

Still another fact remains true. It is possible for a person to become what he visualizes that he can become. As a goal to be achieved, make a mental picture of what you want to become. Keep this goal before you, remembering the Bible injunction, "As a man thinketh in his heart so is he."

The author has used simple criteria by which to judge his basic objectives. *First, I want to know that the objective will be good for me. Second, that it will be helpful to others whom I expect to help me accomplish it. Third, I examine every objective of my life to see if they are hurtful to any.* If I find that my objective in life will help me, be beneficial to others and hurtful to none, then I will go for it.

Once you have your goal set, get this objective firmly fixed in your mind. It is important that you let it constantly speak to you. Since this objective is the image of what you want to become, to make it real you must follow after it. Work toward it. Like an automatic pilot, your projected image will get you there, if you are willing to pay the price.

When you are certain about where you are going and what you want to be when you get there, you must become just as certain about how you plan to do it. The fellow was right who said that "the world will step aside and let pass the person who knows where he is going and how he plans to get there." Beware of desire without action. Balaam had a desire to die like a righteous man, but he was not willing to do anything about it. Therefore his death was not that of a righteous man.

Once your objective is fixed, don't think how you can't; *think how you can.* It is certainly true that if you think you can't, you are right. You can't. But if you think you can, you are right, because you can.

So you won't be detoured from your goal in life, it perhaps would help you to adopt the slogan that Paul used for his life. It was, "This one thing I do."

To accomplish your purpose in life, you should capitalize on every available asset. Not many people achieve their purpose in life alone. Truly, the Bible statement is apropos: "No man liveth unto himself and no man dieth unto himself." You, too, will need help in achieving your goal, and it is available. Other persons will follow and help any person who is worthy and who champions a commendable cause.

When choosing friends or helpers in your cause, be sure that you secure people who will be assets and not liabilities. Some people inspire and lift up, while others depress and hurt your spirit. Some people make you happy when you see them coming while others make you happy when they leave. Your companions will make or break you. Be careful in choosing your friends and helpers.

It is imperative to live in a healthy climate. You may have to guard it from wrong-spirited people. While we drank coffee together one morning, one of my neighbor pastors asked the director of his Sunday School what he thought the temperature of their church was. To his amazement the deacon said, "Pastor, if you want to know the temperature of our church, then put the thermometer into your own mouth. For when you are up, we are up, and when you are down, we are down." Oh, how true this is. To drive forward toward your goal, you must see that a good climate is maintained—at all cost. You may have to maintain this spirit yourself. Others may help or hurt you at this point.

Take your pencil and open your dictionary to the word failure. Cross it out. Completely obliterate the word "failure" from your vocabulary. Make up your mind that you will not be a quitter. *Faithful is the word!*

Abraham Lincoln is a good example. If Abe had been a quitter, he never would have become President of the United States. For several years, failures far outnumbered his successes. Hundreds of times Thomas Edison failed before he achieved his objective. It was after his ten thousandth experiment that Mr. Edison succeeded in making a talking machine that said, "Mary had a little lamb."

Is it a fair and reasonable question for me to ask? Will this world lose some of its worth while you are in it, because you take more from it than you are willing to give it?

Someone has said that if there is a secret to success, it is doing the things you know you should do. Would you agree that thirty-six words summarize the greatest life ever lived on earth? They are these: "Jesus the author and finisher of our faith; who for the joy that was set before him endured the cross, despising the shame, and is set down at the right hand of the throne of God" (Heb. 12:2). Perhaps the life of the second most successful man ever to live on this earth is summed up in sixteen words: "I have fought a good fight, I have finished my course, I have kept the faith" (2 Tim. 4:7).

Beginnings are so crucial. If you are going to cross the street or the country, you must begin your journey with a first step. A person can never better himself or his condition until he sets for himself a specific goal, marks out the direction to it, and begins working toward its achievement.

Only in recent years have high-rise buildings been allowed in the city where I live. Several have been erected the last few years. Each year some company attempts to build at least one story higher than any previous building. It is intriguing to note the structure of the foundations of these buildings. When we see a thirty-five story building going up, we know that the foundation was not structured to hold a fifteen story building. The same is true in life. No life can be successfully and happily lived without an adequate foundation.

To the apostle Paul, Jesus Christ was and is the only adequate foundation on which to structure a life. He said, "To be found in Christ not having mine own righteousness, which is of the law, but that which is through the faith of Christ, the righteousness which is of God by faith." When this can be true of you, then you will have a new purpose for living. Your life will have glorious meaning and direction. You will have something to share. What you have to tell, others will want to hear. This kind of witness can come only from an actual first-hand experience, not hearsay.

No building is complete with only the foundation and neither is a life full-grown with only this initial experience. You must refuse to remain *where* and *as* you are. Babies are not born full-grown, and neither are Christians. Growth requires time and effort.

Nothing could be more misleading than for a person to assume that his initial experience of salvation guarantees automatic Christian growth. And it is just as erroneous for a person to believe that to set a basic objective for his life will guarantee an automatic achievement of that goal.

Self-improvement is possible, but people must do it one step at a time. This must become an obsession with a person if he is to make the most out of life. What would you like to be? What do you want to become?

A thermometer can only measure the temperature–thermostats control it. Some people are content to be a thermometer. Other people aren't willing just to measure temperature–they control it. Which had you rather be–a thermostat or a thermometer? There are people who are content to live in circumstances as they are, while others change the circumstances and make them what they desire. Still some say, "Man, I want to be free to do my thing." Too often the person who says this is mistaking freedom for license. There is a vast difference in freedom and license. Those who take liberty to mean license have missed the truth a mile.

Life is a sacred trust, and it stands to reason that it must operate within some bounds, limits, laws, or guidelines. Some aren't willing to accept this fact. "We want freedom," they yell. Some cry, "Freedom," when they don't know what freedom is. Goethe said, "None are more hopelessly enslaved as those who falsely believe they are free." The apostle Paul had a sensible word to say about freedom. He said, "For you were called to freedom, brethren, only do not use your freedom as an opportunity for the flesh" (Gal. 5:13). Under the guise of license, don't abuse freedom. You see, liberty is Christian. License is not Christian. Liberty is always at a price. Liberty that comes from freedom calls upon persons to "love thy neighbor as thyself."

Airplanes are at liberty to fly, but within certain limitations. They are at their best cruising at a proper altitude assigned from some control tower. Trains are free to run, but trains have their limitations. They must run on a track. There is nothing more worthless than a train off the track or a grounded plane that was made to fly. My car is free to make 55 miles an hour in some zones. It is made for the highway, but it is of much less value when it is off the pavement. These could be applied to our lives as parables. Have you made every effort to discover the factors that could contribute to your life's being all that it is capable of becoming?

THE PERSON YOU ARE BECOMING

Now one other word: "It is not by might; it is not by power, but it is by my Spirit saith the Lord of hosts." To work toward one's goal in the flesh, he will end up with what the works of the flesh can reward. But to work toward your objective in the power of the Holy Spirit, you can accomplish what God can do.

Before the invention of the automobile, taxis were drawn by horses. Most places in the city of Macon, Georgia, one horse could pull the carriage. But there was one steep incline that one horse could not make alone. A stable was erected at the foot of the hill, where an extra horse was kept in the event he was needed to hitch alongside the other horse to make it up the hill. This extra horse, used only in emergencies, became known as the "grace horse." He was there to do what the other could not do alone. This could be a parable of your life. Even with a well established objective and a workable plan of action, the time comes when you must have the help of the Holy Spirit. He is always ready to help you.

As you have read the lives of the characters presented in this book, you have readily discovered the ones that let circumstances control them. On the other hand, it is easy to pick out the characters that made the circumstances around them what they were.

To them, life was what they made it. It didn't have to happen the way it did to anyone of them. They made it happen. So it is with you. If you are a normal person, you, too, will be responsible for what you become and do. This book has been more suggestive than exhaustive. What you think most important, you may not have found in the book.

It's not easy coming face to face . . . with yourself. It's sometimes disillusioning and frightening. But it can become an exhilarating adventure.

Rebekah . . . Caleb . . . Samson . . . Saul . . . Lot's wife . . . Jacob . . . the Shunammite woman . . . Samuel . . . Balaam . . . the woman at Jacob's well . . . Judas Iscariot . . . and YOU!

ABOUT THE AUTHOR

Dr. Charles L. McKay is professor of Bible at California Baptist College, Riverside, California. Although past 65, he is "retired" in name only but continues an active career of preaching and teaching. He is one of Southern Baptists' best-known personalities.

He has served his denomination in a number of key capacities—as pastor, as consultant with the Baptist Sunday School Board, as state executive secretary-treasurer, and as professor.

Before going to California Baptist College, Dr. McKay was serving as pastor of the First Southern Baptist Church of Scottsdale, Arizona. Prior to Scottsdale, he had been executive secretary-treasurer for the Arizona Baptist Convention. Before that he was director of enlargement and evangelism in the Sunday School Department of the Baptist Sunday School Board, Nashville, Tennessee.

One of Dr. McKay's most significant contributions to Baptist life was his work with the "30,000 Movement" and "Million More in '54" campaigns, which he helped spearhead throughout the nation.

His pastorates have been in Mississippi, Louisiana, and Alabama.

Dr. McKay has written five books prior to *Face to Face . . . with Yourself.* Two of his best-known are *The Spirit-filled Steward* and *The Call of the Harvest.*

BROADMAN BOOKS TO INSPIRE YOU

From Here to Maturity by John Ishee

Here is a book which contains many practical helps for personal growth. It assists the reader in understanding himself better–and then in building a personality that is positive and victorious.

How to Be Nervous and Enjoy It by Roger H. Crook

Does the title sound unlikely? Nearly every person has his share of "nerves." But these nerves need not defeat a person. Roger Crook shows how you can live with your nerves, understand them, and channel them for creative, dynamic living.

Say Hello to Yourself by Walter N. Wilson

Here is one for youth and youth leadership. It relates Christian principles to transactional analysis–the philosophy of *I'm OK–You're OK.* Wilson is a counselor and teacher of youth. He helps the reader to feel better about himself and shows how to get along better with others.

Survival Kit for the Stranded by William L. Self
with Carolyn Self

Do you feel disillusioned or frustrated or hedged-in? *Survival Kit for the Stranded* is for you. It offers you hope in the midst of a highly technical, confused, messed-up society.

When All the Bridges Are Down by Ida Nelle Hollaway

Share in Mrs. Hollaway's venture of coming back from defeat, frustration, and despair. You will feel with her. Your life will be enriched by making this round trip journey.

BROADMAN BOOKS ARE LIFE-CHANGING, TRUTH-FILLED, AND ENRICHINGLY CHALLENGING.